Three Socialist Plays:
Lear, Roots, Serjeant Musgrave's Dance

Open Guides to Literature

Series Editor: Graham Martin (Professor of Literature,
The Open University)

Titles in the Series

Richard Bradford: *Paradise Lost*
Angus Calder: Byron
Jenni Calder: *Animal Farm* and *1984*
Walford Davies: Dylan Thomas
Roger Day: Larkin
Peter Faulkner: Yeats
Anthony Fothergill: *Heart of Darkness*
P.N. Furbank: Pound
Brean Hammond: *Gulliver's Travels*
Graham Holderness: *Hamlet*
Graham Holderness: *Women in Love*
Graham Holderness: *Wuthering Heights*
Jeannette King: *Jane Eyre*
Robyn Marsack: Sylvia Plath
Graham Martin: *Great Expectations*
Pam Morris: *Bleak House*
David B. Pirie: Shelley
Gareth Roberts: *The Faerie Queene*
Robert Shaughnessy: Three Socialist Plays
Jeremy Tambling: Narrative and Ideology
Jeremy Tambling: What is Literary Language?
Ronald Tamplin: Seamus Heaney
Dennis Walder: Ted Hughes
Roderick Watson: MacDiarmid
Ruth Whittaker: *Tristram Shandy*

ROBERT SHAUGHNESSY

Three Socialist Plays: Lear, Roots, Serjeant Musgrave's Dance

Open University Press
Buckingham · Philadelphia

Open University Press
Celtic Court
22 Ballmoor
Buckingham
MK18 1XW

and
1900 Frost Road, Suite 101
Bristol, PA 19007, USA

First Published 1992

A catalogue record of this book is available from the British Library

Library of Congress Cataloging-in-Publication Data

Shaughnessy, Robert, 1962–
    Three socialist plays – Lear, Roots, Serjeant Musgrave's dance / by
Robert Shaughnessy.
        p.   cm. – (Open guides to literature)
    Includes bibliographical references and index.
    ISBN 0-335-09607-7 (hb)   ISBN 0-335-09606-9 (pb)
    1. English drama – 20th century – History and criticism.
    2. Socialism and literature – Great Britain – History – 20th century.
    3. Lear, King (Legendary character), in literature.   4. Arden, John,
Serjeant Musgrave's dance.   5. Wesker, Arnold, 1932–   Roots.
    6. Bond, Edward.   Lear.   I. Title.   II. Series.
    PR739.S62S52   1992
    822.009 – dc20   91-46580
                                                                        CIP

Typeset by Best-set Typesetter Ltd., Hong Kong
Printed in Great Britain by J.W. Arrowsmith Ltd., Bristol

For my parents

Contents

Series Editor's Preface

The intention of this series is to provide short introductory books about major writers, texts, and literary concepts for students of courses in Higher Education which substantially or wholly involve the study of Literature.

The series adopts a pedagogic approach and style similar to that of Open University material for Literature courses. *Open Guides* aim to inculcate the reading 'skills' which many introductory books in the field tend, mistakenly, to assume that the reader already possesses. They are, in this sense, 'teacherly' texts, planned and written in a manner which will develop in the reader the confidence to undertake further independent study of the topic. They are 'open' in two senses. First, they offer a three-way tutorial exchange between the writer of the *Guide*, the text or texts in question, and the reader. They invite readers to join in an exploratory discussion of texts, concentrating on their key aspects and on the main problems which readers, coming to the texts for the first time, are likely to encounter. The flow of a *Guide* 'discourse' is established by putting questions for the reader to follow up in a tentative and searching spirit, guided by the writer's comments, but not dominated by an over-arching and single-mindedly-pursued argument or evaluation, which itself requires to be 'read'.

Guides are also 'open' in a second sense. They assume that literary texts are 'plural', that there is no end to interpretation, and that it is for the reader to undertake the pleasurable task of discovering meaning and value in such texts. *Guides* seek to provide, in compact form, such relevant biographical, historical and cultural information as bears upon the reading of the text, and they point the reader to a selection of the best available critical discussions of it. They are not in themselves concerned to propose, or to counter, particular readings of the texts, but rather to put *Guide* readers in a position to do that for themselves. Experienced travellers learn to dispense with guides, and so it should be for readers of this series.

This *Open Guide* is best studied in conjunction with the following editions: *Arnold Wesker: Volume One* (Penguin, 1981); *Serjeant Musgrave's Dance*, Methuen Student Edition, ed. Glenda Leeming (Methuen, 1982); and *Lear*, Methuen Student Edition, ed. Patricia Hern (Methuen, 1983).

Graham Martin

Open Guides to Literature: Drama Supplement to Series Editor's Preface

It is no longer possible to regard dramatic literature as exclusively or even primarily a matter of 'literature' or written text. Drama is both text and performance, both literature and theatre, a fact that is increasingly acknowledged both in general criticism and in the more 'applied' discourse of study guides. Ideally drama is best studied in an environment which provides access to live performance and theatrical practice. *Open Guides* to drama proceed by means of directly textual work and discussion, augmented by an address to questions of theatrical realization – theatre history, theatre architecture, staging, design, acting, costume, lighting, audience; and to broader theoretical issues raised by the nature of theatrical art – realism and representation, metadrama, deconstruction, the politics of performance. Each *Guide* presents a stage-centred reading of a text or texts, supported by whatever supplementary material the student may need to open up the performative nature of the dramatic literature in question. In addition brief guidance is provided on how to cope with the most challenging recent criticism and theory, including poststructuralist, feminist, psychoanalytic and semiotic approaches, but focusing in particular on recent developments in theatre history, metadramatic criticism, semiotics of drama, theatre anthropology.

Graham Holderness
Consultant Editor for drama titles in the Open Guides series

Acknowledgements

I am grateful to Graham Holderness for encouraging this book in its formative stages, and for subsequent editorial guidance through the various drafts; to Graham Martin for his comments on the completed manuscript; and to Tim Rhodes for broad-ranging discussions of many of the issues raised here. I am especially indebted to Nikki Goode for her critical acumen and editorial tact, and in particular for reading *Roots* against the grain.

1. Politics and Drama

In this guide we shall be studying three plays: John Arden's *Serjeant Musgrave's Dance*, Arnold Wesker's *Roots*, and Edward Bond's *Lear*. In relation to the last play, we will also be looking at selected scenes of Shakespeare's *King Lear*. There are three major objectives: to engage with the individual texts; to compare and contrast them, exploring shared issues and concerns; and to use the plays as the basis for more general reflections about the nature of socialist theatre.

Taking this last and tricky issue, what *is* socialist theatre? The very words suggest a relationship between art and politics which many people would dispute. How appropriate is it to evaluate a play according to its political standpoint? Can a play, or any work of art, effectively articulate political commitment? And, a most familiar question, can this be compatible with dramatic and artistic merit?

In this chapter we shall be exploring the notion of socialist drama as a category, as a dramatic form, and as a mode of political intervention, through a preliminary examination of John Arden's *Serjeant Musgrave's Dance*. The immediate theatrical appeal of the play seems obvious: strong narrative, vivid characters, violent action and striking and spectacular theatrical set-pieces. Yet many critics, as well as audiences and readers, have been mystified by the play, not least as to what its political message might be: although it is clearly anti-militaristic, it offers no obvious solution to the problem it presents. There is also uncertainty as to where our sympathies are supposed to lie. Other critics have found the play moralizing or didactic: propaganda rather than art. It is as well to be aware of these difficulties before starting: you may have one or other of these responses yourself.

Would you now read through the play, concentrating on the
essentials of the story as if you were experiencing it in the theatre,
but also bearing in mind the following questions:

Should the play be read as 'realistic', or more along the lines of a
fable? Is there a clear moral or message? Does the play have a
central character with whom the audience or reader is able to
identify? Are Arden's intentions primarily artistic or political?

These questions, and your answers to them, form the framework
for the following discussion.

I

Like both Edward Bond and Arnold Wesker, John Arden has
acquired the status of an 'established' playwright, while *Serjeant
Musgrave's Dance* itself has come to be widely accepted as his
masterpiece, a classic of the modern theatre. Since its first production at the Royal Court Theatre, London, in 1959, the play has
been revived on the London stage alone three times: at the Royal
Court in 1965, at the National Theatre in 1981 and at the Old Vic
in 1984 (there was also a BBC television version in 1961). It is a
regular fixture in A-level English Literature and Drama syllabuses,
as well as in higher education drama courses. In its published
form, the play has been reissued not only in the Methuen 'Master
Playwrights' series but also as a student edition, complete with
glossary, explanatory notes, production photographs and critical
introduction; in addition, there is already a substantial body of
commentary and criticism on both Arden and the play itself. All
of these factors seem to indicate that we should see *Serjeant
Musgrave's Dance* as a major play in modern British drama.

But what does this mean? Such accumulation of dramatic and
literary prestige has implications, both political and aesthetic, for
our response to and understanding of the play. How did this play
come to occupy such a privileged position? The play was by no
means as successful when it first appeared. Its first performance
in 1959, as we shall see, provoked responses ranging from the
baffled to the overtly hostile. Such reactions were modified in
retrospect, of course, but they can be useful as a way of identifying the difficulties and critical problems that the play continues to
present to both readers and theatregoers; and it may be that some
of these initial criticisms coincide with your own response. Moreover (and this is of particular importance to the question of
socialist drama), how and why these opinions came to be revised
tells us a great deal about the critical operations that need to

be performed upon a dramatic work – particularly one of a politically provocative nature, like *Serjeant Musgrave's Dance* – for it to achieve 'classic' status.

The first problem appeared to be that of basic comprehension. Some commentators claimed that they found it difficult not only to work out what the play was about, but what sort of play it was, and even whether it was a play at all:

> Why was this piece put on? A play that was anti-Empire and anti-Army would conceivably have its appeal in Sloane Square, but surely not one that was eighty years out of date? If a tract was wanted on those lines it could have been written more persuasively by an intelligent child ... There might have been some felicities of dialogue or wit to leaven this lump of absurdity, but I failed to detect them.[1]

This is an extreme (and, in my opinion, misguided) reaction, but it is consistent with the general response. For many reviewers, the play fell uneasily between the stylized and symbolic techniques of the ballad, social realism and Victorian-style melodrama; the characters were seen as too crudely drawn, with insufficient or inexplicable motives for their behaviour. Thus the reviewer in *The Times*, while admitting that the play contained 'good realistic dialogue' and 'an atmosphere which is mysteriously pregnant with suspense', concluded that 'these dramatic virtues unfortunately get smothered in a mass of character defects'; the play failed by entrusting its message 'to characters who do nothing to win our sympathy'.[2] Other reviewers simply found the play boring, largely because it seemed to offer a moral that was only too obvious; Harold Hobson wrote that it was 'no good at all' for Arden 'to tell us that war is wrong. We know that already. If we are to be told it again, we must be told it entertainingly.'[3] Alan Pryce-Jones of the *Observer*, on the other hand, decided that the play was 'totally nihilist';[4] a view that resurfaced twenty-five years later in one review of the revival of the play at the Old Vic: 'Its colour is unrelieved grey, its conclusion disillusioned, its tone violent and argumentative.'[5]

Even contemporary admirers admitted to its considerable flaws. Again, reservations stemmed from a sense of the inconsistency of the play's tone and style. A. Alvarez, though sympathetic to Arden's objectives, found 'a significant gap between good intentions and effective drama'. There were, in particular, problems of form and style. He suggested that Arden:

> tries to kaleidoscope scenes into each other, sliding from action to introspection and back. But in Mr Arden's hands the method is used merely for its obvious symbolism, not at all for its psychological

insights. Arden's symbols [arise] ... out of the intensity of his own good will. He insists so much on his own meaning that his characters never get a chance to develop. They have simple purposes but no complexity of life, like so many puppets. Even the serjeant's nightmare vision of the end of the world is simply plain oratory, compelling enough as prose sense, but with none of the nakedness, fear and compulsion of a dream. For symbolism to become drama the characters must take charge of the meaning, not *vice versa.*[6]

Problems of style are compounded by those of dramatic construction. It could be said that the play remains static, establishing mood and atmosphere at the expense of plot, until well into Act 2: important information (such as whether Musgrave is genuinely recruiting) is left unnecessarily obscure; while the pivotal event of the killing of Sparky in Act 2 is poorly integrated into the rest of the action and arbitrarily motivated, leading to a hasty denouement in Act 3.

With these considerations in mind, I would ask you now to reexamine your own response to the play on first reading. The main objections to the play can be identified as follows:

1 It is formally uneven and insufficiently unified, hovering between realism and stylization without fully succeeding in integrating them; in particular, the 'poetic' elements are not organically related to character.

2 The narrative lacks momentum.

3 The absence of a sympathetic central character leaves the audience without a clear grasp of the moral and political questions raised.

4 The independent life of the characters and the progression of the action are subordinated both to the symbolism and to the political message.

Do you find that these criticisms coincide with your own response to the play? If so, which strike you as being more convincing? And which of them do you find most relevant to the consideration of the play as socialist drama?

DISCUSSION

All of these criticisms are debatable, and to an extent they could all be said to be subjective responses rather than analytical statements. For our purposes, however, we shall be concerned not so much with the validity of these propositions (which may in any case vary from reader to reader) but with the actual terms of the debate, and with the assumptions underlying it. What I have in mind here is a powerful and pervasive antipathy towards what is often seen as the use of art for political propaganda.

Whatever your initial feelings about the play, most people would probably regard the first two points as less forceful or compelling criticisms than the others. The question of whether the play's dramatic qualities are undermined by its political message is more likely to provoke strong responses, as in many of the first reviews. At the heart of much of the negative criticism of the play is the sense, implicit or explicit, that its pursuit of a didactic purpose is incompatible with dramatic merit.

II

At this point we need to address some of the assumptions, which are both aesthetic and political, conscious and unconscious, informing the criticisms quoted so far. These tend to set the agenda for critical discussion, and may often determine the very questions that can be asked about drama. Many people feel that art and politics do not mix: that using the theatre to promote political aims almost invariably produces propaganda, which is characterized by distortion, exaggeration, oversimplification or 'preaching to the converted'. This objection might be offered as a formal or stylistic criticism, by way of appeal to 'common-sense' criteria concerning drama, art and literature. In this view, propaganda is limited in its concerns, while 'authentic' art is timeless and universal.

Well, is it? Let us examine further some of the preconceptions involved in this critical common sense, for the course of our discussion of socialist drama will involve a reconsideration of some of the basic, self-evident truths about characterization, dramatic form, and the nature and function of drama itself. In short, we need from the outset to challenge critical common sense – a challenge which is itself political.

Read through the following passages. What general assumptions are being made about the nature of theatre in each case? Which is the more political?

> Another frightful ordeal. It is time someone reminded our advanced dramatists that the principal function of the theatre is to give pleasure. It is not the principal function of the theatre to strengthen peace, to improve morality, or to establish a good social system. Churches, international associations, and political parties already exist for those purposes. It is the duty of the theatre, not to make men better, but to render them harmlessly happy.[7]

If Serjeant Musgrave fails in his attempt to bring the war to an end, it is not because I believe such an attempt to be objectively impossible. Indeed I believe it is not only possible but mandatory for citizens in a democracy to use their voices in this cause. The play shows the difficulties involved. They are very great. I myself, alone, do not pretend to be able to solve them. Wars are made by democracies in the name of peace. This I find more sickening than the acts of unashamed aggressors. Our society claims certain virtues. We must act – all of us, as individuals and en masse – as though the claim is true. One man shouting 'No' gets nowhere – millions, whispering it, with diffidence and even with timidity, can make a noise like a tornado. If, at the same time, they act upon that one small word, they will have won.[8]

DISCUSSION

Aren't the two positions diametrically opposed in the art/politics arena? The first passage, which is from Harold Hobson's review of the play, puts forward what purports to be an argument concerned with artistic values, while the second, a statement made by Arden himself, moves rapidly from a consideration of the play as drama to political polemic. Arden is clearly concerned with the usefulness of the theatre within wider strategies of political action, while Hobson urges a disinterested, neutral stance.

Hobson adopts the assured tones of maturity and reason which are characteristic of critical common sense: he asks for politics to be kept out of the dramatic arena. Politically committed drama, like *Serjeant Musgrave's Dance*, fails as art (and as entertainment) because it is attempting to do something for which it is not suited: to 'make men [*sic*] better'. Rather than fulfilling the traditional functions of the theatre, and offering the spectator either the pleasurable escape and reassurance of comedy, or the catharsis of tragedy, it attempts to confront, influence or even *change* its audience. Hobson's judgement offers criticism not only of this particular play but of committed drama in general. The important point is that his argument is couched in ostensibly artistic rather than political terms; he is careful to take issue not with Arden's political position, as he perceives it (an argument which should, in Hobson's view, belong to another context), but with Arden's attempt to promote this through the medium of theatre.

Arden, on the other hand, moves directly from dramatic to political discussion: his view is that it is not just possible for the dramatist to lend her or his voice to political struggle, but imperative. Rather than functioning as a social sedative, drama should be directly and passionately engaged – in an openly partisan fashion – with political issues; such a drama is not one of escapism or reassurance but one of confrontation, intervention and debate. It is a drama that is actively committed to revolutionary political change.

Clearly, such arguments about the nature and function of politics in art (and of art in politics) are central to any discussion of socialist drama; and what you, as a reader, think about these questions will obviously be an important factor. We need to be aware from the outset, however, that here is a clear and fundamental dichotomy: not between a political and a non-political view of drama, or between commitment and neutrality, but between two kinds of politics. The artistic stance is as politically loaded as the polemical one that it criticizes; the argument that drama should avoid moral, social and political intervention because these matters are addressed in another forum is fully as political, in its own way, as the view that drama should take these and other matters on board.

Critical common sense is, as we might expect, firmly entrenched, informing the principles and techniques (as well as the evaluative judgements) of the dominant Anglo-American tradition of dramatic and literary criticism. It is in the very nature of such common sense that it has persisted without being explicitly theorized or coherently formulated: it simply appears as the most 'natural' or obvious way of interpreting drama and literature. Part of the pervasiveness and tenacity of common sense thus derives from the fact that it is not usually recognized to be a political position. It offers a set of literary-critical values which are inseparable from an amorphously-defined liberalism which is itself identifiably political. Broadly speaking, this liberal position (or range of positions) makes virtues of its rational objectivity, its tolerance, and its pluralism; and it rests, ultimately, upon the assumption that there is such a thing as a timeless and universal human nature. Harold Hobson, more overt than most, is at the conservative end of this political spectrum; but his view that political change is something to be left to vaguely defined 'international associations' and 'political parties' is representative of the general liberal perspective. Crucially, political commitment, whether in art or in real life, is seen as illiberal, dogmatic and one-sided extremism, and is consequently regarded with suspicion if not outright hostility.

Although there is a danger here of oversimplifying what is in practice a complex and contradictory range of positions, we can identify and isolate some of its implications for criticism –

questions to be explored more fully in later chapters. In broad terms, however, we can see that the characteristic scepticism and avowed neutrality of liberal criticism has significant political implications. One of its major preoccupations is what it sees as the intractable complexity of human affairs, and the tragic insolubility of recurrent and universal problems. These are often formulated as oppositions: justice versus expediency, the individual versus society, love versus duty, men versus women, and so on. Underlying it all there is a subtle but persistent resigned pessimism about human motives and human behaviour. From this perspective, then, it appears naive and reductive to suggest that we might effect lasting and positive political change, that we make our own history and transform society in the struggle for freedom and justice. Thus the position which perceives itself as transcending politics is in reality nothing of the kind: it actually serves the existing ruling interests very well, acting as a powerful brake against change by encouraging acquiescence in the supposedly inevitable. In this light, the existing social and political order may come to appear both natural and unalterable.

In this way, common sense functions as an *ideology*: not as a coherently or explicitly formulated set of beliefs (the usual meaning of this term), but as a largely unconscious pattern of feeling. This shapes many conventional assumptions about freedom, individual choice and action, as well as about gender, race and class; from these we can construct a picture of the world – the values of the market economy afforded the status of universal truths. This is a far more effective way of ensuring the continuance of the late capitalist system than the more openly coercive means. It is these assumptions that socialist cultural intervention aims to challenge and supplant. There are profound differences between the various socialisms proposed by the three plays we are studying, not only in terms of tactics but of philosophy, and we shall look at some of these differences in the course of our discussion. But they share a common commitment to challenging the idea that a class society organized on the basis of systematic inequalities of wealth and power is either natural or inevitable, necessary or God-given, universal or timeless. As Arden himself put it:

> Mao Tsetung, that succinct poet, has said, 'Whatever the enemy opposes, we must support: whatever the enemy supports, we must oppose.' Or words to that effect ... I recognise as the enemy the fed man, the clothed man, the sheltered man, whose food, clothes, and house are obtained at the expense of the hunger, the nakedness, and the exposure of so many millions of others: and who will allow

anything to be *said*, in books or on the stage, so long as the food, clothes, and house remain undiminished in his possession.[9]

The difference between Harold Hobson's argument and Arden's, and between liberal and conservative criticism and socialist, is thus not between a political and a non-political approach, but between overt and covert politics. Similarly, it can be seen that the difference between socialist and non-socialist drama may not be between propagandist commitment and aesthetic neutrality but between opposing political positions and priorities.

We need to look now at how these common-sense values also offer a set of critical procedures; that is, at how the general perspective is manifested in practice. If the philosophy of liberal and conservative criticism – that genuine art perpetuates the timeless and universal truths of human nature – is a deeply political one, then the battery of techniques that it uses to substantiate this view are equally ideological both in origin and effect.

This may be illustrated by two extracts from Ronald Hayman's liberal critical analysis of *Serjeant Musgrave's Dance*. The first is a commentary on the remarks made by the Earnest Collier in Act 1, Scene 3, comparing the strikers with Musgrave's soldiers (p. 32, from 'Talk to me' to 'These streets is our streets'). The second concerns the characterization of the authority figures in the play.

Walsh, the Earnest Collier, starts off talking very convincingly as a representative member of the group and goes on, not at all convincingly, as a mouthpiece for what Arden wants the play to say ... It's very easy to sympathise with Arden's feelings and to respect him for thinking and caring more than most of us do about rebels shot down in streets, but it's difficult to accept this statement as coming from a collier, who surely couldn't be as aware as this about the punitive expeditions or talk like this about shooting men down in the streets. Cyprus is casting too long a shadow here. It would be interesting to know more about how much anti-imperialist feeling there was in the unions at the time but Arden wasn't concerned to go into that or the question of how Walsh came to be so well-informed.[10]

The Mayor and the Parson are pathetically unconvincing in their big scenes because Arden is only interested in what they do, not at all in what they are. The Mayor is made to be the Unscrupulous Employer, the man who locks his labourers out and pretends that they're striking, the man who uses his public office for his private ends, carrying the Parson and the Constable with him on a tide of hypocrisy ... these three parts are almost unplayable because the villainy is so trite and the irony so heavy-handed.[11]

On what dramatic grounds does Hayman criticize Arden's writing? Does this dramatic criticism also put forward a political position? Do you find his arguments persuasive?

DISCUSSION

Once again we are presented with aesthetic rather than political criticism. The problem, as Hayman sees it, is essentially one of realism: the politically astute collier, able to articulate the contrast between the actions of the strikers and the work of the soldiers, is seen as a dramatic implausibility. There is a lapse in the writing and the characterization, Hayman suggests, because Arden is allowing his 'message' to overwhelm his imaginative objectivity. But is it appropriate to evaluate characters in this play in terms of being 'convincing'? Or to call for historical corroboration of trade-union 'anti-imperialist feeling' when the play is defined by Arden himself as 'an unhistorical parable'? These questions will be considered in greater detail in Chapters 3 and 4, where the relevance of realist criteria are discussed; the key point here is the appeal to common sense – the supposedly self-evident 'truth' about how colliers are supposed to think and behave. In short, Arden's portrayal is judged inaccurate because it conflicts with the universal and obvious truth that the working class is inert and stupid. The result is that this dramatic criticism serves to undermine the credibility of Arden's political point about the interdependence between capitalist and colonial power and oppression.

In the second passage, the question of characterization is not only one of verisimilitude; it is also one of the degree of empathy that the writer is seen to display towards the character. Again, the sense is that the picture of the world presented in the play does not correspond with what Hayman 'knows' to be true – even if we remember that strike-breaking is hardly the figment of a paranoid socialist imagination but rather a reality of industrial struggle. Arden's supposed insensitivity to the complexities of human motive is also attributable to the naivety of socialism. The dichotomy that Hayman invokes between 'what they are' and 'what they do' is an important one, and one to which we will return in later chapters. Here it seems to indicate the difference between a sympathetic and a critical portrayal, which we might also see as a difference of perspective. Whether characters are defined by what they do or by what they are implies that personal empathy is also political. It depends upon where you stand: certainly from the Collier's position it is the actions, not the motives, of these figures of authority that count.

There is an aesthetic and political principle at work here which might be characterized as one of *balance*. The traditional liberal position sees this as crucially important to the authentic work of art, which should succeed in making the disparate, and possibly conflicting, elements of the work cohere to form a harmonious, synthetic unity. The idea of formal unity and integrity is a central consideration in this study; but for the present it is enough to draw attention to its political subtext. It is not difficult to see that this aesthetic priority is directly analogous to the consensual approach advocated within liberal politics. In effect, Hayman calls for just such a balance and impartiality, suggesting that Arden should have been as 'fair' in his portrayal of the oppressors as of the oppressed. In the interests of artistic balance, Hayman invokes the characteristic liberal objectivity which, taking all sides of the question into account, aims at either a reconciliation of class conflict or a discreet withdrawal from it. Either way, the interests of the ruling class are preserved.

III

We can now return to one of the questions posed at the beginning of this chapter. How do we account for the presence of this play, and the others studied in this book, on the academic syllabus? What has happened to them in order for them to become assimilated into the respectable mainstream tradition? This clearly has centrally important implications for our readings of the plays. One of the ways in which the dominant cultural and critical institutions are able to absorb politically subversive material (like this play, perhaps) is to separate conventionally recognizable dramatic virtues from political content. In this respect, much has been made of the 'poetic' quality of the language of *Serjeant Musgrave's Dance*, and its links with the English ballad tradition and method (this is the strategy adopted by critics such as John Russell Brown[12] and by Andrew Kennedy[13]); a formal approach which allows the play to be depoliticized and hence redeemed as a 'safe' literary and dramatic classic. But it is also possible to reread socialist plays in such a way as to confirm rather than challenge the conservative picture of the world constructed by common sense. In the case of *Serjeant Musgrave's Dance*, this is achieved through the dilemma posed by the play itself, and how it is interpreted. At the centre of the play is the question of whether it is possible to break the cycle of violence, and how this might be achieved: the paradox is that Musgrave confronts militarism by an equivalent show of force. The play suggests, first, that Musgrave's solution will simply perpetuate the cycle, and second, that the failure of his attempt returns the town to the situation at the beginning of the play; this is dramatized in the image of the colliers and the dragoons joining hands in a circle, with Annie clutching Billy's skeleton in the centre. How are we to respond to this image? Does the play end with a political – and therefore *soluble* – impasse, or with a more abstract, timeless one, an inevitable consequence of selfish and destructive human nature?

How you answer this question very much depends upon the political and critical perspective that you bring to bear on the text. So far in this discussion we have been considering *Serjeant Musgrave's Dance* as an example of how the socialist play can conflict with the dominant values of liberal criticism; but you may feel that the play itself does not fit all that comfortably into the category of avowedly socialist drama. It may be that its central concerns are not framed in political terms at all. This has been a matter of critical disagreement, which we will now briefly consider.

In the light of the above discussion, compare the following accounts of Arden's politics. Which seems to you to reflect most accurately the play's moral and political stance? How do you account for the disparity between them, and does reference to Arden's stated intentions in his introduction to the play help settle the dispute?

Arden permits himself, in his treatment of the characters and situations in his plays, to be less influenced by moral preconceptions than any other writer in the British theatre today. Hence the difficulty. His work would be perfectly easy for audiences if he attacked morality; that would be shocking . . . it would be 'provocative', and most important of all it would imply by categorically rejecting certain standards that these standards nevertheless existed – there would still be clear, dramatic blacks and whites, even if they did not always come in the expected places. But instead, and much more puzzlingly, he recognizes an infinitude of moral standards, all with their claims to consideration and all quite distinct from the individuals who hold them and try, more or less imperfectly, to put them into practice . . . for behind Arden's work there seems to be brooding one basic principle: not exactly the obvious one that today there are no causes – that would be altogether facile, and in any case just not true – but that there are too many.[14]

At intervals John Arden has been compared with Bertolt Brecht. Both playwrights realize their dramatic conflicts in terms of social situations and pressures, rather than in emotional or spiritual developments. But where Brecht sets forth the moral, the 'message' of his plays, however controversial, contradictory or infuriating that moral may seem, Arden's even-handed exposition of motives leaves his audience without even a disputable guideline.[15]

Even at that stage [1959], when Arden's political consciousness was more intuitive than intellectualised, the problems were framed by a socialist rather than a liberal perspective ... Arden's basically dialectical approach became increasingly clear (certainly in retrospect though surprisingly not to many critics at the time) in his early masterpiece *Serjeant Musgrave's Dance* ... though the play was set in an unspecified historical period, it was about the results of an imperialist war waged by a capitalist society, and clear connections were drawn between capitalist economics and war ... These were the political terms of reference of Arden's early plays. And they were so explicit that it is hard to understand how the plays could ever have been taken as anything other than profoundly political. But they were.[16]

DISCUSSION

The first two accounts of Arden's political philosophy and dramatic method emphatically repudiate the 'propagandist' charge made in some of the first reviews of *Serjeant Musgrave's Dance*. In opposition to this, both stress what they see as Arden's avoidance of didacticism, suggesting that he is detached and objective – the antithesis, that is, of the presumed conventional socialist playwright. Arden is thus reclaimed from propaganda for art. In contrast, the third account attempts to trace a continuity of socialist analysis and commitment in Arden's work in the context of the development of revolutionary socialist theatre in Britain in the 1960s and 1970s; it attributes to the play a definite Marxist politics that the other accounts praise it for avoiding. On one side, then, neutrality and detachment; on the other, commitment.

One way of settling critical disagreements of this kind might be to refer to the author's intentions. Arden's views are set out in his introduction to the published edition, which aimed to answer criticisms of the play's first production. The idea that Arden's position is one of neutrality and detachment, that he intended to be even-handed in his treatment of the conflicting moral and political claims presented in the play, looks unconvincing in the light of Arden's clearly stated position of 'complete pacificism'. If Arden's view is in any way 'objective', it is in its cautiousness and pragmatism, which reflects his recognition of the difficulties involved in putting principle into practice. This is hardly liberal detachment, but rather an awareness of contradiction and complexity; it is not neutral. But although the force of Arden's conviction is not in doubt, it is less clear that the play advocates a specifically socialist or Marxist solution to the problems it poses.

It might be better to see the position as moral rather than political (supposing it were possible to separate morality from politics): Arden points out that the play does not 'advocate bloody revolution'. But this still does not resolve the problems of meaning and interpretation that the play presents. Intended or not, the connections between the economic struggle, imperialism and war are in the text, and may be acknowledged or ignored; even if the play was not written as a consciously revolutionary socialist drama, it can certainly be read – and produced – as one. It is doubtful, in fact, whether the views or intentions of the writer can be seen as either explanatory or authoritative as regards the range of meanings that a play may generate; *Serjeant Musgrave's Dance* seems to escape the initial intentions of the author. Arden was in fact subsequently to reject the moral doctrine of absolute non-violence that he urges here, by moving to embrace an explicitly revolutionary socialism (which necessarily involved accepting the tactical necessity of insurrectionary force). It was this political decision, finally, that provided the resolution of both the unresolved tension in Arden's stated position and the dilemma posed by the play.

This sense of unresolved contradiction that the play leaves us with provides the clue as to both why it has come to be accepted as a modern classic and why it can simultaneously be treated as revolutionary drama. One way of looking at this is to consider whether the situation at the end of the play is to be seen in terms of a *tragic* or a *dialectical* contradiction. The ambiguity and ambivalence that informs the play can be reinterpreted as expressing the sense of hopeless acquiescence in the status quo which we have already seen to be central to the liberal aesthetic and philosophy: the problem of violence is thus insoluble, the play tragic. On the other hand, the refusal to resolve the contradictions shifts this responsibility on to the spectators, encouraging them to effect the concrete political change that will resolve them in the real world. It is here that we can identify the fundamental difference of aims and effects between the drama that dominates the liberal and conservative tradition and the theatre of revolution: one depicts the problems of society and human nature as natural, inevitable and insoluble, the other as human-made and therefore amenable to solution – through the socialist transformation of society. Bertolt Brecht, who as the major twentieth-century theorist and practitioner of socialist drama will feature recurrently in our discussion, has formulated this difference in terms of the distinction between the Epic and the Dramatic Theatres (a distinction which is discussed in more detail in Chapter 3). For the present, it is enough simply to listen to the responses of their respective spectators:

> The dramatic theatre's spectator says: Yes, I have felt like that too – just like me – It's only natural – It'll never change – The sufferings of this man appal me, because they are inescapable – That's great art; it all seems the most obvious thing in the world – I weep when they weep, I laugh when they laugh.
>
> The epic theatre's spectator says: I'd never have thought it – That's not the way – That's extraordinary, hardly believable – It's got to stop – The sufferings of this man appal me, because they are unnecessary – That's great art: nothing obvious in it – I laugh when they weep, I weep when they laugh.[17]

Which of these responses seem appropriate to *Serjeant Musgrave's Dance*? However we read it, we are left to answer in reality the question which ends the play: 'D'you reckon we can start an orchard?' Yes or no?

2. Text and Performance

In the previous chapter we considered the range of possible meanings that a dramatic text may have, with regard to its politics. Here I want to explore further this idea of diversity in relation to the specific problems – and pleasures – that we experience with the *dramatic* text; that is, to understand the specific nature of texts which are designated for theatrical performance. You may have already noticed differences of emphasis between the critical judgements of *Serjeant Musgrave's Dance* based on a viewing in the theatre and those derived from a reading of the play; it is easy to forget that the plays we are studying existed as *theatre* before they became *literature*. Our concern here will be with how the reading of a play can recover its theatrical potential, can move from text to the real or imagined dimension of performance. The emphasis will be upon how you, the reader, might actively produce theatrical meaning, either in your imagination or in practical production. There are two aspects to this: the awareness of dimensions of meaning beyond the spoken words on the page, conveyed through the non-verbal elements of theatrical communication, and the recognition that theatrical meaning and effect are essentially dynamic and multi-dimensional. The basis for this discussion will be the first scene of the second of our selected texts, Edward Bond's *Lear*.

I

What is unique about reading a playtext as opposed to, say, a novel or a poem? Possibly you will have read the three plays without seeing this as a problem. Entering the imaginative world of a play necessarily involves staging it, however impressionistically, in the mind's eye – rather like reading a novel, which is the form which provides the bulk of our reading experience. And if we turn to the first scene of *Lear* a preliminary reading conveys the bare narrative clearly enough. To the extent that we actively engage in mentally visualizing the dramatic fiction from the clues that are offered by the text, we are producing it. But because this process is often largely unconscious, it can underestimate the playtext's actual and potential range. Certainly, when we compare the information given in *Lear* with the narrative and descriptive techniques of a novel, it appears pretty sparse. There is a tendency to concentrate upon what seems on the page to be the chief source of dramatic meaning, the dialogue – which also constitutes the play's 'literary' quality. As we shall see, this narrowing of focus has important implications for critical interpretation and analysis. In performance, however, the spoken word may not always be paramount or authoritative: there are other elements of dramatic communication at work, elements which may amplify and reinforce, or undermine and contradict, the verbal meaning. Our first priority as readers, therefore, is to be receptive to the clues that the text provides as to its non-verbal dimensions, to recognize them and render them concrete. The objective is to construct a rich, detailed and informed performance text.

Written stage directions provide a starting point. Playtexts vary in both the nature and the degree of information provided in the form of explicit directions; you may have noticed particular differences between the three texts being studied. The comparative detail of *Roots* is itself significant in formal terms, and is explored in the next chapter. For the moment, we shall concentrate upon how the first scene of *Lear* invites us to construct a complex, dynamic theatrical narrative. Let us consider first the visual signals indicated by the opening and subsequent stage directions. This means taking account of the elements of both *setting* and *action*. In the first category are the set, properties and costumes; in the second are grouping, movement and gesture. Alternatively, we can divide these into elements which the actors *use* and those which they *do*. We shall take them in turns, remembering that the categories are neither rigid nor exclusive.

Read through the scene, noting down any significant details of setting, properties and costume. How do these establish environment, atmosphere and context for the action?

DISCUSSION

You will probably have noticed that the text is very sparing with information about setting, atmosphere and so on. The setting of the scene is indicative rather than descriptive – all we are told about its location is that the scene takes place 'near the wall'. We might imagine an open, empty space; the sole scenic element is the stack of building materials. The use of minimal, carefully selected props to provide a clear theatrical focus for a scene, is characteristic of Bond's technique, which can be described as *emblematic*. We see this throughout the play: a solitary plate and jug in Act 1, Scene 5, a bare lightbulb and a bucket in Act 2, Scene 6. The simplicity is both precise and suggestive. The stack of building materials acts as a visual shorthand for the construction work off stage, and also establishes a *working* environment as the site of significant action: this is important to the mood and atmosphere at the beginning of the play. The sight of the tools that are used in strenuous physical work evokes a hard, utilitarian (we could say very masculine) world. There is also a strong feeling of physical discomfort and danger. The selection of props is closely linked to key words in the dialogue. Repeated references to earth, mud, digging and water suggest a landscape – references which are substantiated by the tarpaulin and the map carried by the Old Councillor (in the original Royal Court production of the play, Lear's party carried umbrellas).

The working environment contains another element: the presence of the military. The only props necessary to the scene apart from the building tools, the tarpaulin and the map are the rifles carried by the firing squad and the Officer's pistol appropriated by Lear. It is a telling combination. The appearance of the soldier issuing orders to the workers in the opening moments alerts the audience: this is a violently authoritarian and possibly unstable society. The polite formality of Lear's walkabout (described by the director of the Royal Court production as 'like the Royal Family today visiting a shipyard'[1]) is counterpointed by the ominous presence of the soldiers. The costuming for the scene, which must be deduced from the setting and action, presents sharp juxtapositions of class and status: the muddy, dusty clothes of the labourers alongside the military uniforms and the costumes of the Royal Family. Already it is possible to see in this visual contrast a cross-section of an entire society, and an introduction to the world of the play.

Now consider what is indicated about the grouping of characters, movement and gesture. How do they relate to the verbal meanings given in text? Look in particular at the relationships between the workers and authority figures.

DISCUSSION

For such a short scene, there is a lot of violent action and a large number of characters. On the page, the swift succession of events may be confusing or chaotic. But in theatrical terms, the action is carefully orchestrated. Where, when and how characters move, for example, communicates power and status; in general, a given character's authority is demonstrated through his control of another's movement. The first appearance of the workers with the body is hasty, perhaps panicky, building to an almost farcical pace as, directed by the soldier and the foreman, they frantically attempt to conceal the corpse. With the mass entry of Lear, Bodice, Fontanelle and the rest, the tempo undergoes an abrupt shift: the workers now move slowly and deliberately, attempting to convey an impression of normality. Lear's authority at the beginning of the scene could be suggested by placing him still centre-stage while the subordinate characters move around him: he points to the tarpaulin concealing the dead worker and Warrington and the soldier go to lift it. Lear remarks upon the slowness of the firing squad and is then himself requested (or ordered) to move out of their way.

Gesture is often richly suggestive: here it communicates power and status. The relatively subordinate status of the workers and soldiers is conveyed by the amount of sheer physical work we see them carry out (the First and Second Workers lugging the body of the dead worker, for example). In this scene, gesture ranges from the formal to the coercive and confrontational: Bodice shaking the Engineer's hand, Warrington's signal to continue work, the Foreman and the Soldier pushing the Third Worker, Lear threatening the firing squad with the pistol. One specified repeated gesture seems especially significant: pointing. The Foreman points to the tarpaulin to cover the dead body; Lear points to it when he asks what is underneath it; Warrington points to the Foreman as witness of the accident; Lear points to the Third Worker as he is tied to the post, and then points the pistol at him and shoots him. The repetition of the gesture offers a connecting motif: the pointing finger is an index of power.

But it is in the grouping that the scene's visual stagecraft works most strikingly. The arrangement and positioning of figures on the stage is emblematic, creating theatrical meaning through juxtaposition and counterpoint. Two examples will illustrate this. First, there is the image around which the scene is structured: the Third Worker, tied to a post, awaiting execution by firing squad, while Lear confronts his daughters across the stage. As he gives the order to shoot, Lear stands in the line of fire, an image which neatly combines visual comedy, a sense of impending disaster and precise symbolism, 'ironically illustrating the implicit confusion and the self-destructive consequences of his ideology, and foreshadowing his own fate as a victim of the wall at the end of the play'.[2] Second, the overall shape of the scene is symmetrical, as the one corpse brought on to the stage at the beginning is multiplied to two at the end. This also foreshadows the final scene, and Lear's body dumped at the foot of the wall.

II

So far we have considered the *visual* performance text. But there is also an *aural* dimension: we must hear as well as see. We may see this in terms of both the sound effects indicated in the stage directions and hearing the words on the page as spoken dialogue.

1 Turn back to the scene, considering it for explicit and implicit indicators about non-verbal sound effects. How do these sounds contribute to the overall meaning of the scene?
2 Read through the dialogue (aloud, if possible), trying to 'hear' it as concretely as you can. What clues are there in the text as to how it should be spoken? How are qualities such as tone, pitch, loudness, and so on, overlaid on verbal meaning?

DISCUSSION

1 The play begins with an empty stage and silence, and then a crash and shouts off stage. Throughout the scene we hear running and marching feet, rifles being loaded and cocked, and, at its climax, a gunshot. The opening sound cues establish tone and atmosphere. How long to maintain the silence, how loud to make the crash, how distinguishable to render the shouts; all these are decisions to be left to the performers; but the overall effect is to create tension, a sense of impending violence. The mysterious noises off are immediately followed by a theatrically compelling visual image – the workers carrying the corpse onto the stage. The aural assault is sustained through the scene. The culmination is the pistol shot, where it forms both a powerful climax to Lear's speech and a brutally ironic counterpoint to his claim that 'I loved and cared for all my children'. But there are other implicit sound effects: the noise of the dragging tarpaulin, the scrape and clank of wood and metal tools, marching feet, rifles being loaded. These sounds contribute to the overall pattern and underscore the dialogue. Finally, in addition to the effects indicated in the text, the theatrical producer might wish to overlay the action with others, musical or atmospheric. The 1982 Royal Shakespeare Company production, for example, accompanied each act of violence with musical sound effects (Bond himself disapproved of this decision, complaining that 'they gave the production some of the spurious thrill of a Hollywood film'[3]) and interspersed the sound of wind between scenes in order to create an 'epic' atmosphere.

2 Although Bond does not, in general, supply stage directions indicating how the text is to be spoken, the overall tone seems to be combative and confrontational: terse, harsh, violent. The gunshot that forms the violent climax to Lear's speech in front of the firing squad powerfully integrates sound and dialogue. The moment has been prepared for through the rising violence of the dialogue itself. The confrontational nature of the exchanges between Bodice and Fontanelle, Lear and other characters in the first scene gives a general sense of how the text is to be spoken; but we can evaluate its workings more closely by investigating some of its semantic and rhetorical strategies as dramatic dialogue. There are some general rules which can be applied here. First, in moving from seeing the verbal text as written to hearing it as spoken, we need to place it in *context*, envisaging also a speech's reception by, and effect upon, those to whom it is addressed: we need to imagine not only the speakers but also the

listeners. We might take into account the presence of silent characters who on stage may make a significant contribution to theatrical meaning. How, for example, do the other characters on
stage, both individually and collectively, react to Lear's tirades? In
silence or not? The Third Worker provides a particularly striking
example of a silent character who may make a powerful impact
on stage. Tethered before the firing squad, he is a silent but
conspicuously visible figure for nearly four pages of dialogue –
why is he silent? Does he remain so voluntarily or has he been
gagged to stifle cries of protest? Or does he perhaps faint from
fear?

The dialogue can be seen as a dynamic sequence of *speech
acts*: the spoken word has a tangible presence and impact in
space and time. One way of assessing the impact of an individual
utterance or a speech is to consider the extent to which it establishes or redefines relationships between characters. In this scene
the dialogue can be roughly categorized in terms of statements,
requests and orders: it is immediately apparent from the text
that the amount that falls into the final category is considerable.
In itself this tells us not only about the prevailing tone of the
scene but also something about the authoritarian nature of Lear's
society (and it is, of course, Lear who issues most of the orders).
Take, for example, the opening lines:

> *First Worker*: Get some water! He needs water.
> *Foreman*: He's dead.
> *Soldier*: Move 'im then!
> *Foreman*: Get his legs.
> *Soldier (to Foreman)*: Can yer see 'em? Look an' see! They're comin'
> up the ditch on the other side.

The dramatic tension derives from the rapid succession of conflicting imperatives, as the workers simultaneously attempt to deal
with the body, remove it from sight, and keep their eyes on the
royal party off stage. The terseness with which orders are issued
indicates social relationships based on coercion and riven by conflict. This continues throughout the scene; and the speed and
frequency with which decisions are made and orders are given
contributes to the overall sense of arbitrary and dangerous power.

We have already seen how key words in the dialogue are used
to indicate a sense of place and physical environment. This is an
instance of a fundamental theatrical technique; one which some
dramatic theorists have called *deixis*, or, more simply, the '*I*
addressing a *you here* and *now*.'[4] Speech between characters is
located in time and space by the use of pronouns and indexical

markers ('this', 'that', etc.). In the exchange between the First and
Third Workers, the Foreman and the Soldier, the structure of
relations is visible in the use of pronouns alone:

> *Third Worker (coming on)*: I shouted to *him* to run.
> *Foreman (coming downstage)*: Go back, go back! Work!
> *Fourth Worker goes off again.*
> *Third Worker*: *You* heard *me* shout!
> *First Worker*: *He* says *he's* dead.
> *Foreman*: Work!
> *Soldier (to First Worker)*: *You!* – make *yerself* responsible for
>   'andin' in '*is* pick t' stores (*Suddenly he sees something off stage
>   and runs down to the others.*) Cover '*im*! Quick!

One thing you might notice here (and throughout the play) is that
the first person singular is used by characters when they are
attempting either to assert or to justify themselves (Lear himself
uses 'I' particularly frequently). It is characteristic of Bond's
dramatic technique, however, that the dialogue centres primarily
around the 'he' that designates the Dead Worker – seen both as
object and human – and that relationships between characters are
organized around this focal point. This connects with spatial and
gestural deixis, as, for example, in the dialogue that follows the
entrance of the royal party:

> *Bodice (to Fontanelle)*: We needn't go on. We can see the end.
> *Engineer*: The chalk ends *here*. We'll move faster now.
> *Councillor (looking at his map)*: Isn't it a swamp on *this* map?
> *Fontanelle (to Bodice)*: My feet are wet.
> *Lear (points to tarpaulin)*: What's *that*?
> *Engineer*: Materials for the –
> *Warrington (to Foreman)*: Who is *it*?
> *Foreman*: Workman.
> *Warrington*: What?
> *Foreman*: Accident, sir.
> *Lear*: Who left *that* wood in the mud?

The deictic references to the 'here' of the landscape and 'this' map
are linked: the map is an emblem of the economic and political
power arising from ownership of the land. A similar connection is
made deictically in the references first to the 'who' or 'what' lies
under the tarpaulin, and then to the wood lying in the mud: the
impersonal nature of the deixis, whereby the Worker's body is
literally objectified, is appropriate to a social system which treats
its subjects as mere raw material.

These, then, are some of the ways in which the text fashions
speech as dialogue and action. The above close reading should, I
hope, bring out the detailed basis from which the more imme-

diately observable verbal effects of the text arise. Hearing the text as spoken, other effects are apparent. The meaning of the verbal text is, of course, mediated via the characteristics of the speaking voice, the *paralinguistic* features of the utterance. Some of these effects are suggested in the text. Part of the meaning of the exchanges between Lear and Bodice and Fontanelle, for example, might derive from the antiphony between the male and female voice; Lear's patriarchal authority could be suggested by the capacity of his voice to occupy time and space. We have already noted how the pistol shot forms a climax to the verbal violence of Lear's speech, which builds in speed, volume and intensity to this point; we may also see it as an aural emblem (linked with the off-stage crash that sets the action in motion) of a persistent brutality exercised verbally throughout the scene. In all, we may consider pitch, timbre, rhythm, speed of delivery, and volume all to be significant elements of dramatic communication.

III

The 'openness' of the dramatic text as a quasi-literary artefact means that the reader must imaginatively or actually supply the additional information in terms of movement, gesture, grouping, sound and so on; in Raymond Williams's words, 'the text does no more than prescribe an *effect*, of which the *means* must be worked out in performance'.[5] All readings, and all performances, thus actively produce textual meaning; and the relations between them are dynamic and often unpredictable: even the performance text that you construct in one reading of the play may radically differ from the next as you envisage alternative possibilities.

So far I have been indicating how impressions gained from a reading of the text as a literary work may be rendered more detailed, more solid and more coherent by making the imaginative effort of transforming them into specific, practicable options for performance. To this extent, then, the active reading of the first scene of *Lear* can make it both richer and more comprehensible; in particular, we can see how words and action interrelate in a complex theatrical dialectic. You may feel, however, that our close, theatrically orientated reading of the scene raises as many questions as it answers. In our close attention to solid imaginative realization, some puzzling ambiguities may become all the more evident. In particular, details which can remain hazy in an ordinary reading of the text become more problematic when they have to become more fixed and specific in theatrical terms. As an example, let us take the costuming, which has already been dis-

cussed as a good way of illuminating differences in social status.
But let us try and be more historically and socially specific. **What
clues are there in the text as to the historical, geographical and
cultural setting of the play? Do they send out contradictory
signals?**

DISCUSSION

We may start with the general expectations we are likely to have
when first picking up the text or sitting in the theatre waiting for
the play to begin. The play's title, of course, invokes Shakespeare's
King Lear (how and why the play does this is discussed in more
detail in Chapter 5); and, according to our degree of familiarity
with Shakespeare's work in general and that play in particular,
we might imagine a vaguely Shakespearian milieu: a Renaissance,
pre-Renaissance or feudal world. The rather cryptic note given
above the castlist in the published text seems to reinforce this
impression:

> According to ancient chronicles Lear lived about the year 3100 after
> the creation. He was king for 60 years. He built Leicester and was
> buried under the River Soar. His father was killed while trying to fly
> over London. His youngest daughter killed herself when she fell
> from power.

This brief account is taken from the chronicles written by
Geoffrey of Monmouth and Holinshed, the medieval and
Renaissance historians who were among the sources used by
Shakespeare. The setting would thus appear to be much the same
as in his play: a pre-Christian Britain which is largely mythical
(the bizarre detail of the Icarus-like fate of Lear's father reinforces
this). We are told that Lear is a 'king', leading us to expect some
sort of primitive monarchy.

And yet when we turn to the play these expectations are
immediately confounded: from the beginning the action seems to
be located in the contemporary world (building materials, rifles
and pistols). The first figures to appear represent the proletariat
rather than the peasantry: they are workers, not serfs – yet they
exist in conditions of feudal subservience. The names of some
of the characters – Warrington, Cornwall, North – suggest an
English setting (as does the dialect of the First Soldier), but it is an
England with its own Great Wall. There is an ambiguity about
some of the names themselves – is Warrington a name or a title?
What are we to make of a name like Fontanelle? (According to the
Oxford English Dictionary the word means 'the top of a baby's

skull'). Especially when there are also characters called Ben, Thomas and Susan? Lear is described as a king and behaves simultaneously as a feudal despot and a contemporary politician. The world of *Lear* is one with both flogging and firing squads, with photography but apparently without telephones. The action is both mythical and commonplace: the construction of the wall belongs to a world of epic narrative but it is carried out by navvies and engineers. The setting is 'timeless', but in a disturbing rather than a reassuring sense: there is a troubling and inexplicable feeling of dislocation, anachronism and contradiction about the action and the world of the play.

The reader, assimilating these conflicting signals, may be able to construct a conventionally coherent, if eclectic, image of the world of the play; but in the theatre the contradictions may be emphatic and disconcerting. In order to make sense of these contradictions we need to examine in more detail the particular mode of theatre that Bond is attempting to create. At the very least we might deduce that the dramatic method of the play is not what we normally define as 'realism', the form which dominates the mainstream of contemporary drama. This leads us to the subject matter of the next chapter.

3. Form and Meaning

In the first two chapters our discussion of the relationship between drama and politics has raised questions about the nature of dramatic communication. In this chapter I wish to explore these questions further by examining the relationship between form and content, or between the ideas of the play and the means of representing them. Our starting point for this discussion is the third of the selected texts, Arnold Wesker's *Roots*. As a play written in the naturalistic mode, it represents the dramatic norm from which both *Lear* and *Serjeant Musgrave's Dance* depart.

I

Arnold Wesker prefaces the published edition of *Roots* with a
note to actors and producers defining the style of the play: 'My
people are not caricatures. They are real (though fiction), and if
they are played as caricatures the point of all these plays will be
lost.'

**In the light of the questions raised in the previous two chapters,
how do you understand the terms 'caricature' and 'real' here? In
what other senses might these terms be used?**

DISCUSSION

The primary sense of the word 'caricature', taken from the visual
arts, is a stylistic one: it refers to a method of selection and
exaggeration of personal idiosyncrasies, usually for the purposes
of satire or parody. But this also suggests the idea of imbalance or
distortion, of representing reality – or of constructing an argument
– from a sectarian position.

Wesker brings together modes of representation – the realistic
and the didactic – which, as we have seen in Chapter 1, are
frequently seen as antithetical. He suggests, on the one hand, that
his plays attempt to faithfully depict objective reality; on the
other, that such representation has a didactic purpose, a 'point'.
The recording of reality coincides with the analysis of it; and the
ideas are to emerge indirectly and obliquely from the action. In his
distinction between caricature and the 'real', Wesker also implies
that there is a necessary equation between dramatic and political
balance and objectivity. The relationship between form and content is thus constructed in terms of the double sense of the word
'realism', which (as we have seen in Chapter 1) in its everyday
use means both a method of representation and a pragmatic,
'common-sense' attitude of mind. This double meaning is not
accidental: the one is often seen as the obvious corollary of the
other. In this way, then, the realist form strives towards an 'objective' and empirical mode of representation which is also 'natural':
it appears, that is, to correspond to what we know of reality itself.

We can analyse how this relationship between form, content
and ideas operates by a close reading of Wesker's means and
effects: how the play creates and sustains a convincing picture
of reality (or 'slice of life'), how it holds the attention of the
audience, and how it develops a political analysis. **Read the first
act of *Roots*, and then answer the following questions:**

1 What means are used to establish a convincing picture of reality? You may find it useful to compare Wesker's Act 1 with the first scenes of *Serjeant Musgrave's Dance* and *Lear*.
2 Can you identify elements of pattern, rhythm and structure that give the action a theatrically satisfying pace, development and unity?
3 Bearing in mind the 'Author's Note' that is found on p. 7 of *The Wesker Trilogy*, what are the key 'ideas' communicated in the act, and how do they relate to the form of representation?

DISCUSSION

1 You will probably feel that the degree of realism is closely related to the amount and quality of detail, in the setting, in the action and in the dialogue. The effect of eavesdropping on real life seems to be enhanced by the inconsequential or 'undramatic' quality of the action, which is dominated by casual chat and domestic routine.

The workings of realism can be difficult to analyse; this is indeed part of its effect. In order to create the illusion of reality on stage, the artifice sustaining it needs to be invisible, or at least transparent. If the technique of the dramatist or the conventions of representation are too visible they interfere with the necessary suspension of disbelief, and hence with the seamlessness and naturalness of the picture of reality. Ideally, the spectator of the realist play should be encouraged to temporarily suspend her or his awareness of being in a theatre.

To a large extent, the integrity of this illusion is dependent upon the achievement of a synthesis, a unity of setting, dialogue and action. It might be useful, then, to isolate these constituent elements in terms of their specific communicative and suggestive effects. From the quantity and quality of the stage directions alone, we can see that the physical environment created on stage is a key factor in theatrical communication. The first thing we may note is the precise geographical location (contrast this with the opening settings of the other two plays). This is a cue for the designer and director: most productions of the play attempt to evoke the harsh landscape of the Fens. We are also told the month and hence the season: it is September. The context is rural, but hardly the setting for a pastoral idyll. This is confirmed by the description of the kitchen/living room. There are few amenities: no running water, gas or electricity. The stove is either wood- or coal-fired; lighting is provided by Tilley lamps; water is drawn by hand. The furniture provides little comfort: it is 'cheap and old'; the room is strewn with washing, papers and discarded toys. We might say that this is, in traditional terms, a 'feminine' milieu.

From these clues we can begin to construct a detailed picture of the play's domestic and social world. The important thing is that it is suggested through concrete details; Jenny Beales singing 'a recent pop song' (a means of locating the action in time) while washing up, and Jimmy Beales wheeling his bike into the kitchen, contribute to the impression of everyday routine. The setting, moreover, is not merely a static backcloth to the action but a dynamic element within it. The characters are not only placed in or against the setting: they interact with and use it throughout the play. Most of the action in this act, as in the whole play, centres on domestic labour. It opens with Jenny washing up, Jimmy's and then Beatie's arrival, and supper ('naturally' carnivorous: liver and onions); it moves through baking bread, cleaning and more washing up; it then ends with all three retiring to bed.

As for action, the act contains little that we might describe as 'theatrical' or 'dramatic': even the appearance of the trouserless Stan Mann (which might elsewhere be a moment of high farce) is understated. The strongest image is that of Beatie standing on a chair with her fist raised; but this is conspicuously at odds with the predominant tone and atmosphere of mundane domesticity. Indeed, the impression of real life derives from the consistently low-key manner in which everyday actions are carried out: it is as if the text carefully eschews more obviously theatrical means of holding the audience's attention. In conjunction with this, the dialogue, which incorporates lengthy silences, reflects the inconsequential, circular and episodic quality of real-life conversation. Apart from a briefly heated political discussion between Jimmy and Beatie in the middle of the act the conversation drifts from one subject to the next: from Jimmy's gut-ache to food to Beatie's relationship with Ronnie, from Mrs Bryant to Stan Mann to Beatie's artistic aspirations. Interspersed are Ronnie's opinions, relayed via Beatie, on work, politics, sex and culture.

The irregularities of the dialogue, and the scrupulous depiction of daily routine, suggest an absence of intervention by the dramatist in his material: reality is not being manipulated but faithfully recorded. The refusal to edit out what might conventionally appear as theatrically irrelevant or potentially tedious becomes a guarantee of accuracy and objectivity. The authenticity of the representation, and hence of Wesker's implicit 'message', is thus authoritatively empirical – derived from observation rather than theory.

2 The primary structuring device of the act is, I would suggest, the dialogue: the rhythm and pattern are mainly dictated by a series of one-to-one encounters. The central unifying motif of the act may be that of 'arrival', structured around a succession of entrances and exits. Although the immediate effect is to create the illusion of eavesdropping upon a 'slice of life' (as if the spectator were looking in upon a room with its fourth wall removed), it is obvious that this is produced through careful contrivance; indeed, what makes the action theatrically engaging and gives it a dramatic logic and shape is the selection and organization of the constituent elements. Both dialogue and action operate plausibly within the parameters of character and situation; in this sense it has the logic and consistency of an objective reconstruction. Entrances and exits, the rituals of the meal and of domestic labour, provide clear focal points around which the dialogue is structured and establish a rhythm and a pattern for the play as a whole. The talk also manages subtly and economically to convey significant information about both on- and off-stage characters. The antagonism between Jimmy and Jenny is communicated not only through the terse, combative dialogue but also through their physical separateness on the stage; while the recurrent references to Mrs Bryant in the dialogue, although she is not to appear until Act 2, establish her very early on as a powerful presence in the play.

The apparently episodic quality of the action and inconsequentiality of the dialogue is actually carefully patterned. This is partially provided by the progession of time, as the stage grows darker and lamps are lit; there is a pattern also in the ordering and reordering of the set and props. The lighting of the lamps coincides with Beatie's suggestion that they tidy up the room; when Jenny produces a loaf of bread from the oven, they begin to do so. The visual chaos of the beginning of the act is transformed to neatness and order at the end. A further means of structuring the action is in the arrangement of entrances and exits and consequent permutations of characters. The pattern is based on twos and threes, with Beatie at the centre. The arrival of Stan Mann towards the end of the act is the only point where there are four characters on stage. This asymmetry reflects the character's disruptive function in the drama, where he acts as a challenge to the complacency of the others. Act 2 adopts a parallel structure, where the intrusion of a fourth character – Healey – brings the news of Stan's death. The establishment of a rhythm of arrivals prepares for the non-appearance of Ronnie in Act 3. Throughout the act, as through the play, the preparation and consumption of food is pivotal to the interaction between characters: communal feeding embodies domestic harmony. Women play traditionally nurturing roles, while food becomes literally a prop sustaining the fragile equilibrium of familial unity. Ironically, the diet of platitudes and empty rituals upon which the Beales and Bryants subsist starves them of genuine emotional nourishment – as the periodic plaintive eruptions of 'guts-ache' indicate.[1]

3 There are two points in the act where political 'ideas' are directly discussed in the dialogue: the account of the arguments between Beatie and Ronnie about language and articulacy, and the discussion of the transport workers' strike. We've seen that reading a play, as opposed to seeing it performed, can cause the spoken word to sound more direct, unequivocal and (Wesker's term) 'pompously' authoritative than the theatrical context might warrant. The play's 'message' may thus be detached from character and situation, from the 'physical business of living'. Effectively this is a disruption of realism, as characters lose their credibility, complexity and autonomy, the illusion of independent life, to ventriloquize the author's views. This is particularly pertinent to *Roots*, in that its 'point' appears ready-made in Beatie's quotation of Ronnie (at least in Act 1: as the play progresses the ideas become more Beatie's own). The key question is whether these ideas are spoken in character, or whether they can be readily identified with the views of the author; that is, whether Beatie, and Ronnie, act as mouthpieces for the political message of the play.

On the page – if only because of the sheer length of Beatie's monologues – it appears that her viewpoint, and that of the absent Ronnie, are to some extent privileged and authoritative. The discussion of language and culture, which is a central concern of the play, is set out clearly and mostly uninterrupted. Beatie is given space to develop the point that articulacy is central to personal and political liberation; there is a sense in which this is a 'set speech', a point to be taken not only by the characters on stage but by the audience as well. A similar sense inflects the discussion of the transport strike and farm workers' wages (which itself turns to a discussion of education and culture): is Jimmy merely a dramatic and political stooge, a sounding-board for Beatie's/Wesker's views on workers' solidarity?

Wesker takes some steps to prevent this. Although the audience is often invited to agree with Ronnie's views, the fact that they are mediated through Beatie also ironizes and distances. Beatie's unremitting capacity to quote him verbatim might be dramatically awkward, but it is at least given a basis in her character; moreover, the fact that Beatie *is* Ronnie's acolyte for much of the action is very much an issue. Generally, when Beatie begins to lecture the other characters, they will point this out, which not only to some extent fulfils the requirements of realism but also sustains a dialectic. Mrs Bryant's remark towards the end of Act 2 that Ronnie 'talk[s] like a book' counterpoints the mannered artifice of his pontifications against spontaneous utterance, and goes some way towards deflating his pretensions. Both Beatie and Ronnie are sufficiently unattractive to prevent the audience from regarding them with unqualified approval: Ronnie may be idealistic but he is also pompous; Beatie's enthusiasm contains a considerable element of insensitivity, and their shared enthusiasm to improve others has a marked arrogance. As Irving Wardle put it in a review of the 1978 revival of the play: 'your antipathies are fairly evenly divided between the bovine family, Beatie's bossy parrot cries, and the intellectual prig in the background.'[2] The refusal to heroize the central character is an aspect of realistic technique, as well as being one of the means of creating a dialectic in the play.

There is, none the less, a tension in the play between its ideas and the form it utilizes to convey them. For Wesker, the vitality and force of the political argument derives from the synthesis of theory and reality, rendering socialism part of the 'physical business of living'. In this sense the dramatic technique of the play successfully relates form to content: concrete details of living and working, meticulously reproduced, are interwoven with an argument about socialism and culture which might otherwise appear rather abstract; the argument of the play cannot be separated from its dramatic context. But it is an unstable synthesis; and the instability is at the very heart of the dramatic form.

Although *Roots* has been praised for its scrupulous realism, many critics have still found it both implausible (particularly in Beatie's last-act epiphany) and didactic. **Read these critical responses to the play, and then consider the following questions:**

> This is distinctly a 'message' play and the audience loved its downright mixture of earthy humour, stylised characterisation and preaching ... It may seem churlish to carp about a play written with an urgent sincerity about a basic dilemma, but it fails to convince largely because it veers a little too crudely between polemics and nose-to-the-ground farmyard 'life'.[3]

> [Wesker's] plays suffer from the way he uses them to plug the message ... If only he had been content to write a more documentary and less didactic play, he might have written a great play.[4]

These farm-labourers are a stagey lot. In fact they're not really
characters but abstractions ... The idea expressed in 'Roots', that
intellectual curiosity is a good thing, is valid enough, though unexceptional. But plays, like poetry, are not made of ideas alone. Just
as language is the principal ingredient of poetry, so characters are
what is needed for drama ... much of it seems like an animated
Workers' Educational Association lecture.[5]

How do you account for these responses? Can you detect any
similarities with the criticisms of *Serjeant Musgrave's Dance* discussed in Chapter 1?

DISCUSSION

These comments reflect the tendency of traditional criticism to
label as didactic or polemical any drama which offers an even
mildly positive account of socialism; similar attacks, as we saw in
Chapter 1, were directed at *Serjeant Musgrave's Dance*. Objectivity is set against commitment, complexity of character against
ideology, entertainment against ideas. Here, however, the problems of form and style that complicated the response to *Serjeant
Musgrave's Dance* do not arise. Wesker has written a conventionally, but imperfectly, realist play. This may seem surprising in
view of the above discussion; but once again we can see an
essentially political response to the play articulated as formal or
stylistic criticism. Ideologically, this is implicated in the term
'realism': the authenticity of the representation is evaluated within
the framework of common sense. This dictates, as it did in Ronald
Hayman's response to the colliers in *Serjeant Musgrave's Dance*,
that workers are unable to mount a socialist analysis of their
conditions of life, still less that they might articulate it.

At this point it is necessary for some terms to be more closely
defined. So far in the discussion I have applied the term *realism* to
the dominant mode of representation within *Roots*. In its broadest
sense, realism is the form which dominates the majority of the
modes of contemporary drama, from the television soap opera to
the West End thriller. What unites these disparate forms is the
manufacturing of illusion; for the duration of the performance the
spectator suspends disbelief and accepts the synthesis of character,
action and setting as a replica of reality. But *Roots* may be located
within a more specific mode of realism: Naturalism. The terms are
often treated as if they were interchangeable, but Naturalism
indicates a combination of dramatic form and method and a
philosophical and political outlook that is not necessarily characteristic of the realist mode as a whole.

Some historical contextualization is required here. The Naturalist movement in the European theatre was a development of the late nineteenth century, exemplified by the plays of Émile Zola and August Strindberg, and culminating in the work of Henrik Ibsen and Anton Chekhov. In the course of the nineteenth century, the theatre refined the techniques of illusion, with the development of the picture-frame stage and the increasingly sophisticated technology of lighting, sound and scenery appropriate to it. The Naturalist movement aimed to harness these to an attempt to apply scientific method to the drama. The theatre was seen as a laboratory, where human motives, actions and relationships, and the social conditions within which they operated, could be subjected to microscopic scrutiny. The philosophical impetus of this was materialist, the method empiricist and positivist: the term 'naturalist' was itself directly derived from the natural sciences (in particular, it evoked Darwin's theory of natural selection). Its materialism opposed the mysticism and idealism of Romantic drama: as Zola put it, the Naturalist drama aimed to effect 'the gradual substitution of physiological man for metaphysical man'.[6] Raymond Williams points out that materialism and empiricism were fundamental driving forces of Naturalism's very form, which was nothing less than 'quite newly perceived relations between human actions and a material environment':

> To put the point sharply, the major naturalist dramatists did not prescribe a new kind of dramatic scene, the detailed physical realization of a room or some other physical environment on the then qualitatively altered stage, for *technical* reasons, or because new techniques of stage carpentry and lighting made this more feasible. They put on these rooms, prescribed in detail in a new form of writing which was more than mere 'stage direction', because such immediate physical environments were, in their view, necessary elements of the dramatic action. They were, in the fullest sense, *living* rooms: places made to live in in certain ways: environments which both reflected and influenced their possibilities of life.[7]

The sets of Naturalistic drama were, as in *Roots*, almost invariably domestic interiors; they are an emblem of the perceived relationship between the individual and the social world. The domestic space of the Naturalist drama was a political arena, where private actions could be seen in a public context. At its point of emergence, Naturalism offered a critique of bourgeois society which was often seen as scandalous, not least because its uncompromising secularism and its ruthless exposure of middle-class hypocrisies. Ibsen's *A Doll's House* (1879) is a famous example, confronting its audiences with the economically and sexually exploitative nature of the institution of marriage; as is the same author's *Ghosts* (1881), which brought to light the unwelcome fact of the prevalence of syphilis among the respectable bourgeoisie.

Despite this initial capacity for outrage, however, the Naturalist movement eventually proved amenable to assimilation into the mainstream of twentieth-century drama. This was partly due to a dilution of its philosophical content, so that the twin impulses of social and environmental determinism and the (perhaps contradictory) desire for radical political action that were embodied in the drama surrendered to a sense of the naturalness and inevitability of the world that was represented on stage. The obsessive reconstruction of the material environment thus became a source not of disturbance. but of satisfaction. But it was also the result of a formal and political contradiction. The Naturalist movement's greatest limitation, as well as its greatest strength, was that it articulated a critique of bourgeois society while retaining bourgeois man (however critically presented) as the protagonist, as a figure of identification for the spectator and, implicitly, as the agent of possible political change.

I would like you now to consider *Roots* in relation to this tradition. Can we see the form and emphasis of the play as a development of Naturalism? Do you think that its political project is helped or hindered by the form itself? The following passage of commentary by J.L. Styan may help in providing a context:

Between the wars, the London theatre had declined into a mediocrity of quasi-realistic drama. Now [the late 1950s] an eruption of new writing was caused by young dramatists who appeared to return to the roots of realism without so much as a nod to theatrical tradition. Their work was variously identified as 'kitchen sink drama', 'dustbin drama', 'angry theatre', 'committed theatre', and so on. It was variously explained by the aftermath of war and disillusion with the first Labour Party majority in Parliament, by the spirit of 1956, the year of Suez and the Hungarian uprising, by the spirit of rebellion against a feudal structure in Britain. But it was a particular rebellion against the conventional, middle-class fare of the London theatre, especially the verse drama of T.S. Eliot and Christopher Fry. The new drama might be parochial, but it would be a vigorous prose drama of ideas, an attempt to breach the wall which, in Arthur Miller's words, 'seals the British theatre from life'. It would strike hard at one of Britain's cherished cultural institutions, and if this meant forsaking the drawing-room for the kitchen, so be it ... The subjects of the plays struck audiences as new – often the life of the urban or rural working-class, a group which has traditionally been used only as a pool of comic characters ... the well-furnished elegance of the middle-class stage gave place to kitchens and attics, with all their sordid paraphernalia of cooking stoves and ironing boards and beds.[8]

DISCUSSION

Wesker aims to represent working-class rather than bourgeois experience, a progression that is undoubtedly political. In this sense it recovers one of the original aims and methods of the Naturalist movement: the exposure of real social conditions in order to provoke recognition and hence political action. At the same time, though, the shift is primarily in terms of content rather than form.

The idea that the political consciousness of the audience might be raised if it is brought face to face with oppressive social conditions has been a strong one in twentieth-century Naturalism, particularly in Britain and Ireland (in the early plays of George Bernard Shaw and Sean O'Casey, for example). But this strategy of exposure has its limitations. The shift within Naturalism from bourgeois to working-class subject matter certainly alters the emphasis of the political debate, but not necessarily its fundamental terms. If it can be discussed simply as the substitution of one set of rooms, or one set of furnishings, for another (the emblem is kitchen sink rather than french windows), aren't the theatrical and social relationships between individual and environment substantially unaltered? The arena of significant action remains domestic and interpersonal; history and politics are still imagined as vast, imponderable forces which intrude upon private experience. For example, *Roots* argues the need for solidarity between rural and urban workers, but its very form makes this point difficult to dramatize: small wonder that political debate jars in this setting. The domestic space also exerts a powerful pressure towards *reconciliation*: often, literally, by shutting out the external social world. Even the materialism of Naturalist dramaturgy can be appropriated by bourgeois ideology, as mastery of the physical world turns into the commodification of reality. The home environment, however unprepossessing, still has the consolations of ownership: the stage is still furnished with (in both senses of the word) properties. As a microcosm of social relationships, the image of the room fits into the bourgeois privatization of experience.

The attempt to appropriate a traditionally realist form for radical objectives also leaves unchallenged the accepted relationship between stage and audience, with the result that the radical content of the drama comes into conflict with the conditioned response. Far from questioning the self-evident and the familiar, the form encourages the spectator to respond within the framework of common sense. The fact that *Roots* focuses upon the nuclear family, for instance, does not invite critical scrutiny: the family relationships and structure are assumed as natural, the divisions of power and responsibility within this as quite unexceptional. But just how natural is it that the women in the play are perpetually engaged in domestic labour while the men go out to work and drink? Least exceptional is the continued centrality of *character*, conceived within these private and personal parameters (a consideration which receives greater attention in the next chapter). For the present argument, its importance is that it retains the possibility of identification and empathy. Ultimately the play, and the audience, are concerned with what happens to individuals, and their capacity for personal growth. It seems an essentially reformist rather than revolutionary variety of socialism.

II

At this point we may return to *Serjeant Musgrave's Dance*, and to some of the questions raised at the end of Chapter 1. It is, I hope, clear that the negative responses to the play that have already been outlined draw substantially upon the ideological-dramatic values of 'realism' – which involve, in particular, assumptions about the plausibility of character and the integrity of the stage illusion. In this section I wish to focus on this second aspect, and upon its ideological implications. In *Roots*, as we have seen, the political meaning and effect of the play are dependent upon the creation of a detailed and coherent illusion of reality. *Serjeant Musgrave's Dance*, on the other hand, is clearly not Naturalistic. We will now look at the relationship between its form and style and its political content; and in particular its mode of address to the audience. **Would you now please reread Act 3, Scene 1 of the play, and consider the following questions:**

1 **How far is Arden concerned to construct a realistic illusion? What non- and anti-illusionistic devices are there in the scene?**
2 **How is the presence of the audience used as part of the dramatic action and meaning?**

In considering these questions, you should bear in mind Arden's introduction to the play as well as the following passages. The first is from a discussion of the relationship between his own dramatic technique and that of the folk ballad; the second from a description of a pantomime performance:

> In the ballads the colours are primary. Black is for death, and for the coalmines. Red is for murder, and for the soldier's coat the collier puts on to escape from his black. Blue is for the sky and for the sea that parts true love. Green fields are speckled with bright flowers. The seasons are clearly defined. White winter, green spring, golden summer, red autumn. The poets see their people at moments of alarming crisis, comic or tragic. The action goes as in Japanese films – from sitting down everyone suddenly springs into furious running, with no faltering intermediate steps.
>
> What does this mean in terms of the theatre? To start with – costumes, movements, verbal patterns, music, must all be strong, and hard at the edges. If verse is used in the dialogue, it must be nakedly verse as opposed to the surrounding prose, and must never be allowed to droop into casual flaccidities. This is the Brechtian technique, more or less.[9]

> ... an individual dressed as a gorilla bounded on to the stage and did a lot of knockabout with two comedians, and then came leaping off into the audience in a completely hideous gorilla costume, and raced about the audience, plonked himself down into a fat woman's lap and took her hat off, deposited her hat on a bald man, then flung its arms round another bald man and nuzzled him in the face, it was the most extraordinary thing I've ever seen in a theatre ... and just as you began to wonder how far it was going to go the gorilla suddenly bounded back on to the stage, unzipped the costume, and it was an attractive chorus girl in a little dress. And then everybody cheered and clapped. This sort of thing is acceptable in pantomime: people love it. But we haven't got round to taking our pleasures sufficiently casually in the legitimate theatre yet.[10]

DISCUSSION

Like the play as a whole, this scene is drawn in bold terms, which itself emphasizes theatrical artifice. The primary colours of the costumes and the clear-cut quality of the emotions and actions are ballad-like. The setting is minimal: the marketplace is indicated by a single item of scenery in the middle of an otherwise empty stage. Other non-realistic devices include the alternation between verse and prose and the use of song, and the token noises off for crowd responses. Rather than acting as eavesdroppers or observers, the audience is directly involved in the theatrical event, mainly by the actors' use of direct address. In this scene they play the collective role of the townspeople.

The models provided by the ballad and the pantomime

invoke alternative traditions of entertainment to those of the
'legitimate' theatre – the mainstream within which a play like
Roots would appear to be quite comfortable. They also offer a
rationale for the theatrical methods that Arden is using in his play.
We shall consider these two aspects in turn.

If we see the scene (indeed, the whole play) in the strong
primary colours, distinct verbal patterns and vivid images of the
ballad, then the plausibility of the stage illusion in realist terms
perhaps becomes less important than its emblematic quality.
Theatrical meaning is bold and manifest: the audience is presented
with a succession of distinct theatrical images or tableaux. The
scene divides neatly into sections, a series of presentations to both
on-stage and off-stage audiences: the Bargee, the Mayor and
Musgrave. A display of rifle drill, the Gatling gun, and the show-
stopping unveiling of Billy's skeleton and Musgrave's demonic
dance. The skeleton remains hanging throughout the rest of the
scene, as Musgrave and the soldiers confront first the townspeople
and then each other and the Dragoons arrive; the scene ends with
Musgrave and Attercliffe on the forestage, the Bargee and the
Colliers joining hands in a circular dance behind them – and
Annie at the centre of the circle, sitting clutching Billy's skeleton.
The action has a strong and clear rhythm, while grouping and
movement throughout the scene are organized around a series of
linked dialectical oppositions: order versus anarchy, love versus
violence, life versus death.

Although there is a great deal of significant action in this
scene, it is constructed in bold theatrical terms. Visually, verbally
and aurally, the stagecraft relies upon key primary elements used
both economically and suggestively. Notice the epic scale of the
action and the boldness of the theatrical gestures it incorporates: a
public recruiting meeting, confrontations at gunpoint, a skeleton
hauled aloft, dancing. Little space here for subtle nuances, either
in the emotions or in the movement and action: the scene consists
of a series of spectacular *coups de théâtre*, a sequence of striking
dramatic reversals. The result is not confusing, however, because
of the ballad-like simplicity and clarity which structures the
scene. The colour scheme is vivid and resonant: the scarlet of the
soldiers' tunics and the Mayor's robes, the gold of the Mayor's
chain, the black of the Parson's gown and the clothes of the
colliers, the white of Billy's bones. This colour-coding is echoed
through the dialogue:

Lead 'em in with a Holy Book
A golden chain and a scarlet gown.

But white and red
He waves his head

His blood's on my tongue, so hear what it says. A bayonet is a raven's beak. This tunic's a collier's jacket. That scarecrow's a birdcage.

Colour imagery is one of the central organizing principles of the play, in the overall conception of scene and situation (as Hurst puts it earlier in the play, 'on the run, in red uniforms, on a black-and-white coalfield') and in visual and verbal details throughout, from the black, red and white of the playing cards in the opening scene, to the green apple in the final ballad, to the nicknames of the characters themselves: 'blood-red roses', 'bloody lobsters', Black Jack.

As well as a strong visual pattern, the scene has a precise and hard-edged verbal and aural shape. The dominant sound in the scene is the drum beaten by Hurst, which punctuates and under-lines the dialogue, particularly in Musgrave's 'recruitment' routine (p. 83). Other key sounds include the snap of the magazines being loaded, the shot that kills Hurst (accompanied by the blare of a bugle), and, finally, the crashing of feet in the Colliers' dance. The dialogue itself frequently adopts a strong rhythmic pattern, like the patter of music hall comics:

Bargee: He says: 'Who says strikes, it's a bloody lockout.'
Constable: Silence for the Mayor!
Bargee: Silence for His Worship!

There are four songs in the course of the scene. As Arden empha-sizes, these are distinct from the spoken dialogue, embodying an audible shift of register. In each case – the Bargee's fairground barker's ditty and his rendition of 'Michael Finnegan', Musgrave's song during his dance, and Annie's lament over the skeleton – the narrative is interrupted in order to emblematize emotional and political meaning. Together with the visual stagecraft, this tech-nique is described by Arden as 'Brechtian' in the sense that the social content of action is sharply defined in clear, concrete terms. In Brecht's theatrical vocabulary, the method is *gestic* (from *Gestus*), a term which combines the senses of essence (or gist) and gesture. Thus Annie's song combines with her holding up Sparky's torn tunic in a compelling theatrical image, which offers a con-nection between private grief and its political cause.

The ballad-like qualities of this scene are characteristic of the play as a whole: a boldness and simplicity of situation and stage vocabulary, together with a musical patterning and economy. This is one sense in which we might see the play as 'stylized' and non-

illusionistic. But there is another element which we need to take
into account, a way of looking at the play which derives from
Arden's description of the pantomime performance. **Before pro-
ceeding to the following discussion, I would ask you to have
another look at that passage.**
    At first sight the relevance of this anecdote to *Serjeant
Musgrave's Dance* may seem a little obscure. If we are to apply
the model to the play, we need to identify the theatrical conventions within which both operate. Without being unnecessarily
serious, we can make some observations about the theatrical techniques used here that may illuminate Arden's methods. The first
point concerns how we interpret this pantomime performance as a
theatrical spectacle. Quite obviously, neither audience nor performers are concerned with the creation of realistic illusion.
The audience's pleasure depends upon the *unreality*, the absurd
incongruity of the spectacle; the final surprise is when the person
inside the costume turns out to be a girl rather than, as expected, a
man.
    The audience's response to such a spectacle is both simple
and sophisticated. As Albert Hunt points out in a commentary on
this anecdote, questions that would be central to the theatre of
illusion do not arise:

> in the legitimate theatre you would be complaining that the scene
> wasn't 'convincing'. What pretty girl would want to make herself
> look like a gorilla? Or, 'What does this reveal to me about her
> character?' you would ask.[11]

But the comedy is not entirely trivial. The gorilla routine works by
lightly playing with and questioning the audience's customary
sense of reality, in particular its sense of theatrical convention;
also by breaking down the conventional boundaries between
stage, performers and spectator.
    This model is relevant in two respects to *Serjeant Musgrave's
Dance*. The first is the notion of a theatrical sequence which is
structured more as a series of 'turns' than as a realist narrative;
the second is the presence of the audience as an active constituent
of theatrical meaning. Firstly, without pushing the analogy too
far, we can see that the scene we have been studying in particular
does offer a succession of opportunities for virtuoso theatrical
display, probably transgressing the boundaries of verisimilitude.
Musgrave's recruitment routine is itself a piece of theatre. Just as
the pantomime audience admires the consciously displayed skill of
the performers more than the consistency of their characterization,
so in this scene the audience is invited to applaud the actors'

verbal and physical skills, as they recite, sing and dance. What is required of the actors is a larger-than-life, bold, declamatory style that will engage the audience, presenting them with the essentials of the narrative and situation, executed with the clarity, directness and panache of the stand-up comic.

There is another sense in which the play draws upon the pantomime tradition. It has a similar cheerful and populist eclecticism of style and tone, mixing song, speech and action, pathos and slapstick, elements of realism and self-conscious theatricality. The penultimate scene is essentially an elaboration of the basic principles underlying the slapstick routine. If in theatrical terms we see the scene as a series of spectacular set-pieces, we may also see it in dramatic terms as a sequence of equally spectacular juxtapositions and reversals: an army recruitment which is actually a protest against militarism, a demonstration of weapons drill which becomes threatening, a gun turned on the audience, divisions and sudden switches of loyalty. At the eleventh hour, the cavalry arrive, catastrophe is averted, and law and order are restored – but the 'happy ending' is ambiguous, to say the least.

Throughout the scene, the active engagement of the audience is vital. The stage directions at the beginning of the act tell us that speeches are directed 'straight out to the audience', so that the theatre spectators are incorporated in the action as townspeople, with the cheers and boos of the off-stage crowd deliberately 'rather unrealistic'. Arden is playing a game with the boundaries between audience and performers, fiction and reality, which is similar to the game with the pantomime gorilla. The key moment is when Attercliffe turns the Gatling gun to face the audience: its force derives from the spectator simultaneously feeling threatened and detached: the gun is both dangerously close and real, and safely contained within the theatrical fiction. Even as it compels the audience's involvement in the theatrical event, the play emphasizes its make-believe status.

It is evident that all this is designed to evoke a particular type of response, and a different kind of relationship between the audience and the dramatic fiction, to that of the legitimate theatre exemplified by *Roots*. We need now to consider what significance this difference has in political and ideological terms, to discuss why it is important that Arden (and, as we shall see, Bond) utilize a dramatic technique that eschews dramatic illusion.

Much of the foregoing discussion implicitly invokes a model of theatre which is derived from the theory and practice of Brecht (who is cited by Arden himself). At this point I would like to bring Brecht more fully into the discussion, by looking at his summary of the distinctions between the Dramatic and the Epic Theatre (introduced at the end of Chapter 1):[12]

Dramatic Theatre	Epic Theatre
plot	narrative
implicates the spectator in a stage situation	turns the spectator into an observer, but
wears down his capacity for action	arouses his capacity for action
provides him with sensations	forces him to take decisions
experience	picture of the world
the spectator is involved in something	he is made to face something
suggestion	argument
instinctive feelings are preserved	brought to the point of recognition
the spectator is in the thick of it, shares the experience	the spectator stands outside, studies
the human being is taken for granted	the human being is the object of inquiry
he is unalterable	he is alterable and able to alter
eyes on the finish	eyes on the course
one scene makes another	each scene for itself
growth	montage
linear development	in curves
evolutionary determinism	jumps
man as a fixed point	man as a process
thought determines being	social being determines thought
feeling	reason

How do these distinctions between Epic and Dramatic Theatre apply to *Roots* and *Serjeant Musgrave's Dance*? Does the table offer a convincing account of the relationship between form and content in each case?

DISCUSSION

Some of the stylistic and formal distinctions seem clear enough: for example, between the linear and episodic arrangement of scenes. But their projected effects upon the spectator are more arguable: in political and formal terms, the two plays each incorporate elements of both modes of theatre.

   The fundamental principle underlying all of these distinctions is that dramatic form is profoundly ideological; that challenging the dominant ideology necessitates a revolutionary break with the dominant aesthetic. In Brecht's view, the Dramatic Theatre encourages passivity and acquiescence because it confirms what the spectator already 'knows' to be true to experience. The objective of the theatre of illusion (and, in particular, of the Naturalistic theatre) – to persuade the spectator to suspend her or his disbelief and accept the authenticity of what is reproduced on stage – fosters an essentially uncritical attitude. The emphasis of such a theatre is personal and individual rather than social; its material is feelings rather than ideas; it engages the emotions but not the intellect. The methods of the Epic Theatre, conversely, aim to stimulate criticism, reflection and debate, challenging conventional wisdoms instead of assuming or endorsing them. In form and content, the Epic Theatre is dialectical, presenting contradictions in place of synthetic, illusory unity.

You may feel that this dichotomy is too neat if it means identifying *Roots* with the reactionary and conservative Dramatic Theatre. After all, is not Wesker as concerned as Arden (if not more so in this play) with presenting a positive socialist analysis? Does *Roots* not engage the spectator in an argument? Perhaps; but the problem, as we have seen, seems to be that the realist form of the play frames and contains the debate, ultimately curtailing the range and quality of the questions that it is able to ask, and the answers that it is able to suggest. I would urge you to consider the argument in Act 1 between Beatie and Jimmy over the transport strike. Here is the opportunity for the play's focus to move beyond the domestic and interpersonal, to progress from private actions and feelings to collective struggle. But the demands of empathy inevitably confine the significance of the exchange to what it reveals about the individuals involved: Jimmy's stubbornness, or Beatie's insensitivity in 'bringing politics into the house'. This is an apt metaphor for the intrusiveness of the public and the political in relation to the domestic space of the Naturalistic environment. The strike itself is peripheral to the main action, a dramatic conflict that lies in the clash of wills and temperament. Similar difficulties arise at the end of the play, with Beatie's 'epiphany' of self-awareness. Clearly, Wesker invites us to see this as a moment of personal triumph for Beatie and to share the experience of transformation. The problem is that we also forget that Beatie's apotheosis (precipitated by a traditional device, the emotional crisis) is so isolated as to make a nonsense of the play's apparent socialism. We might equally overlook the fact that Beatie's new articulacy is 'exactly what she's been saying all through the play, when she's only been quoting her arty boy

friend'.[13] The humanism of Wesker's play lies partly in its faith in
individual salvation through self-discovery and partly in the moral
that the working class can be taught self-improvement through the
acquisition of 'culture'; there is little doubt that the former aspect
is dramatically more compelling and persuasive. The emotional
catharsis that the play offers is at the expense of a revolutionary
or class solution to the problems it presents, and in this sense it
may be seen to evade the implications of its own critique. We can
interpret the Naturalist preoccupation with mimetic realism in
similar terms: by absorbing the spectator in the coherence and
accuracy of its representation of reality, it excludes alternative
points of view, and, most importantly, the possibility that the
world depicted on the stage is open to political change.

Arden's dramatic technique in *Serjeant Musgrave's Dance* is
not simply avant-garde or stylized for purely experimental aesthetic reasons, but ideologically motivated (although at the time
the play was written Arden would probably not have theorized
his dramatic method in quite the terms set out by Brecht). The
theatrical method of the play is, in the Brechtian sense, one
of *alienation* (from the German *Verfremdungseffekt*) or of de-
familiarizing, making strange, the accepted order of the real. The
aim is that the spectator should be engaged in a dramatized
political analysis rather than speculating about the motives of, or
identifying emotionally with, the 'hero'. Thus the switches from
verse to prose to song, from presentation to re-presentation, are
designed – as in Brecht's theatre – to interrupt the flow of action
and emotion, preserving the critical response. Instead of simply
siding with or against Musgrave (which might be the case in a
theatre of illusion and empathy) the audience is invited to evaluate his actions and the situation within which they take place.
Emotional catharsis is avoided: while the fate of Musgrave and
the soldiers may be individually tragic, the play leaves us with
the impression that what is more important is the possibility of
collective struggle for change.

As Epic Theatre, *Serjeant Musgrave's Dance* requires the
spectator to practise what Brecht called 'complex seeing': she or
he must simultaneously follow the story and reflect upon it, see
the events of the play as real and unreal, engage with both a
dramatic situation and a dialectical argument. This may sound
rather daunting: but in a sense the Epic Theatre calls for a more
basic (more 'natural'?) response than does the illusionist theatre.
What could be more contrived, more unnecessarily taxing, than
the willing suspension of disbelief in an elaborately manufactured

replica of reality? Perhaps complex seeing is not so complex, after all; as Arden points out, popular theatrical traditions like the pantomime frequently deploy a range of alienation effects (from question-and-answer routines to the transvestite conventions of the Principal Boy and the Dame) which audiences are able to accept quite readily; and indeed Arden was in later plays to adopt techniques of popular theatre more wholeheartedly. He also points to the essential simplicity of the ballad form:

> This kind of theatre is easily misunderstood. I have found in my own very tentative experiments that audiences (and particularly critics) find it hard to make the completely simple response to the story that is necessary to appreciate the meaning of the play . . . This does not happen in ballads at their best. There we are given the fable, and we draw our own conclusions.[14]

It is, again, a question of expectations, as to what constitutes 'legitimate' theatrical communication. If we locate the play within the popular tradition, a different set of expectations are operative. Such theatre prefers allegory, fable and parable (*Serjeant Musgrave's Dance* might be seen as all three), forms which in themselves clarify the moral and political issues of the story, lending its events – and social reality itself – strangeness and distance.

III

In this section I wish to turn to *Lear*, and to look at how Edward Bond, following both Brecht and Arden, has developed his own form of Epic Theatre. You may have already found *Lear* to be an Epic play of a rather different order to *Serjeant Musgrave's Dance*; what I aim to do here is to investigate that difference in more detail, by concentrating on one scene in the play that clearly demonstrates Bond's technique.

Would you now please reread Act 2, Scene 6, bearing in mind both the evaluative and ideological criteria of Brecht's table and the methods used by Arden. Does Bond appear to be aiming for an effect which is 'Epic' in the sense we have already discussed?

Do you find the play's technique is closer to conventional realism than that of *Serjeant Musgrave's Dance*? How does it compare to the Naturalistic mode of *Roots*? Bond's play specifies few props – why? What effect does this achieve which contrasts with the extensive use of props in Wesker's play?

DISCUSSION

This scene is representative of how the play as a whole differs from the more disruptive Epic Theatre of *Serjeant Musgrave's Dance*. It has none of that play's telling transitions between prose, verse and song, it lacks the montage effect of switching from narrative to recitative, from enactment to commentary; neither is the audience enlisted as an active collaborator in the action, as in Arden's play. In short, there is none of the populist anarchic or farcical potential that a performance of *Serjeant Musgrave's Dance* might develop.

But Bond's 'realism', if it can be called that, is selective enough to become stylized. Although it is not stated in the stage directions, the scenography of the play is intended to be minimal and emblematic. The action of *Lear* moves from the open countryside to the courtroom to the wall itself; in each case only strictly *necessary* details of scenery are used, so that the stage is often almost completely empty. Although the settings are specific, there is no attempt to construct a complete, convincing environment for each one. In this scene the sole item of scenery is the bare lightbulb. Instead of reproducing an environment which embodies the lives of a small group of individuals, the empty stage is a public arena.

Another way in which the scene, and the play, may be distinguished from Naturalism is in its scale, in the sheer number of characters in the scene. Whereas the rooms of Naturalist drama, as we have seen, enclose private dramas, the cell setting presents personal experience in a public and political context. The scene is typical of the play as a whole in that it features fourteen characters, half of whom only appear here. The play as a whole has eighty speaking parts, registered for the most part not as individuals but in functional and class terms, as workers, soldiers and prisoners. This does not mean, however, that we should see the play in terms of ten developed, complex central characters surrounded by a cast of abstract, symbolic or caricatured supporting characters: the large cast is rather an attempt to place everything that happens in the play in a social context, to show, as Bond puts it, 'the character of a society'.[15] Conventionally, the dramaturgic hierarchy of interest which regulates the degree of complexity and sympathy afforded to principal, leading or major characters and 'walk-on' parts is itself a reflection of the ideological tendency to separate the private self from society, in that it encourages us to perceive heroes and heroines as splendidly isolated individuals. Here each character is defined by and in terms of social situation. The audience is primarily concerned not with how figures think and feel but with what they *do*.

The language of the scene shares some of this functional and emblematic quality – a quality which is itself definable as gestic. In place of the non-sequiturs of Naturalistic dialogue it is concise and to the point. It is language geared towards the exposition of narrative and social situation rather than character or atmosphere.

So far I have emphasized the rational and analytical aspects of Bond's technique, which has affinities with the Epic Theatres of Brecht and Arden. **I would like you now to think about how Bond departs from the previous models. Referring to Brecht's table, there are two aspects of the scene in particular that I would like you to concentrate upon:**

1 **What are your feelings about the violence in this scene, and in the play as a whole?** Bond's Preface to the play is relevant here, as is the distinction he has made between Brecht's alienation effects and his own 'aggro-effects':

> Alienation is vulnerable to the audience's decision about it. Sometimes it is necessary to emotionally commit the audience – which is why I have aggro-effects. Without this the V[*erfremdungs*]-effect can deteriorate into an aesthetic style . . . We need a sort of positive V-effect, something less abstract than V-effect – if V-effect becomes merely the removing of emotional tension so that the object or situation being inspected just, as it were, floats loose.[16]

2 **What significance do you attach to the Ghost? How does it relate to the reality of the rest of the scene?**

DISCUSSION

1 In common with many audiences and readers of the play, you will probably react strongly to the play's depiction of violence. Clearly, it is designed to have an emotional impact on the audience: what is more arguable is whether this effect is simply gratuitous or whether it has a serious artistic and political purpose.

The violence of Bond's plays, and of *Lear* in particular, has always been, in critical terms, a highly contentious issue. His *Saved* (1965) and *Early Morning* (1968) had run into serious difficulties with the theatre censor, the Lord Chamberlain: the former play contained a scene showing a gang stoning a baby to death. *Lear* contains the largest number of acts of violence and brutality in any of Bond's plays to date. Apart from the numerous shootings, the play shows the beating of Warrington and his deafening with knitting needles, the rape of Cordelia

and the goring to death of the Ghost. The cumulative effect has
provoked many of Bond's critics to characterize the violence as so
relentless that it becomes meaningless; one reviewer wrote of the
1982 Royal Shakespeare Company revival that it convinced him
only that there was 'nothing of interest in Mr Bond's plays beyond
their determination to shock'.[17] This scene is a particularly con-
centrated example, containing an off-stage shooting, the shooting
of Fontanelle followed by her autopsy, the bayoneting of Bodice,
and then the blinding of Lear himself. None of these incidents is
distanced by being stylized, and most of them happen in full view
of the audience. The theatrical impact of each act of brutality is
intensified by the calmly efficient manner in which it is performed
(Soldier O calmly fixing a bayonet as Bodice struggles, the Fourth
Prisoner's scientific patter during Lear's blinding) and by the little
details: the lightbulb over the autopsy table, the eyelid clips and
'soothing solution of formaldehyde' incorporated into the blinding
machine.

Are these simply shock tactics – whether crude or sophisticated? The brutality is, after all, hardly implausible; Bond
asserts in his Preface that he sees it as his ethical responsibility as
a writer to comment upon the violence of contemporary capitalist
society. A literary defence might be that acts of violence are inte-
gral to the image structure of the play. The autopsy of Fontanelle,
for example, is a powerful metaphoric expression of a central
philosophical and political issue. Until this moment Lear has
believed that wickedness and cruelty are inherent in human
nature; the exposure of her innards marks the beginning of the
realization that violence is in actuality the result of social injustice.
Lear's initial failure to recognize the body as that of his daughter,
and his wonder at its internal beauty, are themselves metaphoric,
as is the moment when he puts his hands into the corpse: they
enact Lear's growing recognition of his own capacity for destruc-
tion. There is an even greater weight of thematic significance
attached to Lear's blinding. Apart from the mythic resonances inherent in this dramatic motif (deriving primarily from Sophocles'
Oedipus Rex and Shakespeare's *King Lear*, an aspect which will
be discussed in Chapter 5), we can also see it as the theatrical
culmination, the *Gestus*, of a recurrent image of sight and blindness as a metaphor for insight and awareness: in Act 2, Scene 3,
Lear recalls that 'I killed so many people and never looked at one
of their faces' (p. 42), while in Scene 6 he declares that 'I must
open my eyes and see' (p. 60). Bond employs the metaphor not to
suggest transcendent or purely personal insight, but to illustrate
the capacity of power to occlude the consequences of its own

actions; even as it is performed, the Fourth Prisoner's utilitarian rationale for Lear's blinding, detailed in scientific language, is a means of masking the brutality of the act itself. There is a difference, however, between analysing a theatrical effect on the page and responding to it in the theatre. Although my exposition aims to extract the dialectical significance of Bond's stage violence, its effect on the stage is more direct and immediate – that is, sensational and emotional rather than rational and intellectual. This is, of course, the point: aggro-effects shatter the detachment advocated by Brecht, compelling an involvement in the theatrical event which is, at least in the first instance, very much a gut reaction. This is Dramatic, rather than Epic, Theatre: instead of standing outside and studying, the spectator is in the thick of the experience. The question is whether in this instance the aggro-effects are so powerful as to undermine completely the spectator's capacity for rational evaluation. Does Bond take sufficient account of the likely responses of the spectator? Is it, perhaps, not altogether surprising that shock, horror or self-protective frivolity have become the primary defence against the visceral emotional impact of the play?

There is a further point about the play's violence that needs to be briefly considered. This is prompted by William Gaskill's observations concerning his direction of the first production of the play. He records that he 'particularly hated directing' the scene of Warrington's torture:

> It's when you catch yourself saying, 'When you push the needles in his ears could you just be a little more ironical on the doo-dee-doo-dee-doo' that you realise that you're in danger of joining the band of sadists yourself.[18]

The line between the gratuitous and the 'responsible' representation of violence is a difficult one to draw (even supposing such a distinction can be made), as Gaskill's remarks indicate. There is a particular problem with this play, it seems to me, in that the most graphic acts of brutality are inflicted upon women. If the main effect of Fontanelle's evisceration is its metaphoric function, does this not involve reducing the woman's body to a convenient token to provoke (male) insight? Is this in itself a grotesque objectification? This is not to accuse Bond of misogyny but to point out that such representations may have implications, and effects upon the spectator, that escape the intentions of the author. As a final open question, it is perhaps worth thinking about what distinguishes this scene – maybe even the play as a whole – from sadistic pornographic fantasy.

2 The Ghost of the Gravedigger's Boy is clearly symbolic or metaphorical, and as such operates upon a different plane of reality to the rest of the scene. It is one of the central images of the play, together with the wall, the cage and the blinding. Here the role of the Ghost seems to be that of an intermediary between Lear and the audience. This device noticeably distinguishes *Lear* stylistically from the other plays. In terms of dramatic and literary convention he is a rather unusual ghost: first appearing in Lear's cell in Act 2, Scene 2, he deteriorates in the course of the play, becoming increasingly emaciated and dependent upon Lear, acting as a silent witness to the brutalities that occur, and 'dying' for a second time in the penultimate scene.

Let us be clear that there is nothing supernatural about the Ghost: Bond's understanding of reality is unequivocally materialist and humanist. Bond is not suggesting the survival of a soul after death – which would offer the 'realistic' rationale for its appearance. Instead, we see the Ghost in symbolic or metaphorical terms, a theatrical device. But symbolic of what? A figment of Lear's imagination? The audience is seeing what Lear sees himself, a device extended in Act 2, Scene 2, when he is joined by the ghosts of Bodice and Fontanelle as children (who are at this point still alive). The technique is that of the Expressionist theatre, where the stage action and setting embody the psychic conflicts within the protagonist. But this psychological explanation seems inappropriate here, and inadequate to the power and suggestiveness of the device. At this point, and in Lear's interaction with the Ghost throughout, both realism and Lear's internal drama move to the plane of allegory. We should see the Ghost's function in the play as emblematic, as it acts as a focus for empathy (a point discussed further in Chapter 5). Like *Serjeant Musgrave's Dance*, but in a different way, the play demands an attitude of complex seeing, whereby the audience attends to the action on a number of levels simultaneously: realistic, Epic, allegorical and mythic.

This returns us to the questions raised at the end of Chapter 2. The juxtaposition of realism, surrealism and Epic Theatre is comparable with the disturbing and inexplicable anachronisms in the play. As Bond has indicated, these contradictions are crucial to its effect:

> The anachronisms are for the horrible moments in a dream when you know it's a dream but can't help being afraid. The anachronisms must increase and not lessen the seriousness. They are like a debt that has to be paid. Or as if a truth clutched at anything to save itself from drowning.[19]

The world of *Lear* can only exist on a stage. Its contradictions echo the refusal of narrative closure at the end of *Serjeant Musgrave's Dance*; while the simultaneous effect of disorientatingly dreamlike unreality and painfully insistent reality sets the social world against its ideological refraction and distortion. Needless to say, the contradictions that constitute the world of the play are left to be resolved by the audience, in reality.

4. Language and Character

I

A central concern of the previous chapter, in identifying the differences between the theatre of illusion and the Epic Theatre, was on the role of empathy. In principle, the Epic Theatre eschews this form of emotional identification. The spectator's attention is directed towards the social and political basis and significance of action and behaviour, rather than towards purely personal and psychological considerations. In this chapter we will explore this issue in more detail; first, by examining the particular conventions of characterization that are operative in the three texts, and second, by questioning the ideological assumptions inherent in the concept of 'character' itself.

We will begin by looking at *Roots*, which uses clearly recognizable conventional Naturalistic methods of characterization. The aim of the following discussion is not to provide 'character sketches' of the dramatis personae of the play, nor to discuss motivation or emotion in any great depth and detail; it is to identify how character is constructed and communicated.

Consider the character notes given in the stage directions on
pp. 92, 106 and 118. Do they have a particular emphasis? What
does this indicate about the play's method of characterization?

DISCUSSION

The emphasis is upon speech, a primary requirement of realist
drama. 'Natural-sounding' dialogue is a central technique for
establishing character.

The fact that Wesker recurrently draws attention to the
characters' patterns of speech is surely significant. As we might
expect, the substance of the playtext is, in the first instance,
words; the primary resource for the actor and the reader in the
construction of character will necessarily be what she or he says.
Furthermore, we sense that speech is a richer and more suggestive,
as well as a more detailed, means of revealing or embodying the
character's inner life and emotional truth than are, for example,
movement or gesture. Although we can glean something from
action and gesture, what individualizes the people in the play is
what they say and how they say it. In the traditional realist novel,
the writer has access to the characters' thoughts and emotions,
conscious or unconscious, and conveys them to the reader; in a
Naturalistic play, the mediation of this inner life remains indirect
and oblique. Realistic characterization is initially dependent upon
the plausibility of speech: we expect that what is said should first
and foremost be convincingly 'real'. Wesker certainly believes that
verisimilitude in dialogue is a precondition for effective realism:

> I always get annoyed with critics who talk about me being 'a master
> of dialogue'. Well, for Christ's sake, if you're not a master of that,
> what else? This is only a beginning, and shouldn't be the reason why
> a play is good, it's the least that one expects.[1]

Wesker's irritation is understandable; but, then again, the fact that
this ability is seen as noteworthy is an indication not only of the
importance of creating the illusion of real speech in the theatre but
also of its difficulty. Of course, the apparent spontaneity and
naturalness of even the most convincingly realistic dialogue is as
patterned and contrived as anything else in the play. Nevertheless,
the distinctive quality of effective Naturalistic dialogue is its
capacity to suggest the hesitation, the repetition and redundancy,
the circularity and non-sequiturs, of everyday speech. What is
expected, overall, is a degree of consistency between what is said
and the person speaking.

1 Would you now give a close reading to the dialogue between Mrs Bryant and Stan Mann that opens Act 2. How would you describe the pattern, tone and orientation of the conversation? What do we learn from it about the characters of the participants?

2 Compare this with the dialogue that follows between Beatie and Mrs Bryant. What differences are there?

3 Throughout this scene, and through the play as a whole, speech, or the act of speaking, are themselves frequently the subject of comment or discussion. What significance do you attach to this?

DISCUSSION

1 'Gossip' is one of the key words in Wesker's stage directions, and it seems an appropriate term to apply here. The conversation is relaxed, perhaps rather complacent, although Stan Mann emerges as a more vital and imaginative character than Mrs Bryant.

The term 'gossip' implies triviality and aimlessness, a passive and repetitive recounting of events; speech as a mechanical routine. Certainly, much of what passes between Mrs Bryant and Stan here – as elsewhere in the play – would in linguistic terms be defined as 'phatic' communication; that is, the act of speech conducted mainly in order to reinforce existing personal and social contacts rather than to convey new ideas or information. This inconsequentiality is an aspect of the realist technique: the dialogue is not immediately arrestingly 'dramatic' in the sense of advancing the narrative or precipitating conflict or crisis. The predictable and repetitive quality of Stan's utterances, and Mrs Bryant's equally ritualized responses, indicate a long-standing relationship: they have undoubtedly had many such conversations in the past, and phrases such as 'I had my day' and 'Blust' bear the stamp of constant reiteration. The restrictions of the speakers' vocabulary, phraseology and range of subject matter suggest limited horizons on both a social and a personal level – although Stan is depicted as the more lively and imaginative of the two, purely through his tendency to break the conversational rules (as when he addresses Mrs Bryant as Daphne and then offers to 'mount' her). The banal and circular quality of the dialogue (which appeals to actors because it leaves them a lot of space to 'act') signifies a lack of emotional and intellectual commitment to what is said: even Stan's elegy for his youth is rather formulaic.

There is an underlying irony to the whole conversation, in that it turns out to be the last time we see Stan Mann alive (Mrs Bryant: 'I aren't hevin no dead 'uns on me like'). This is in itself a pointed commentary upon the characters. The chief effect, however, is to establish their preoccupation with 'trivia', their avoidance of emotion or thought. The important point is that the characterizations are based on principles of coherence, unity and consistency: a character's speech has a pattern that reliably delineates her or his personality. Plausibility is conditional upon continuity; the inner life of a character is inferred through the *subtext*: the order of meaning that motivates and confers unity upon the words of a part. The term was coined by the late nineteenth-century Russian actor and director Constantin Stanislavsky, a figure whose methods have played a pivotal role in the development of Naturalistic acting techniques. In Stanislavsky's terms, the subtext is:

> the manifest, the inwardly felt expression of a human being in a part, which flows uninterruptedly beneath the words of the text, giving them life and basis for existing. The subtext is a web of innumerable, varied inner patterns inside a play and a part, woven from 'magic ifs', given circumstances, all sorts of figments of the imagination, inner movements, objects of attention, smaller and greater truths and a belief in them, adaptations, adjustments and other similar elements. It is the subtext that makes us say the words we do in a play.[2]

The subtext is the rationale for consistent characterization, and the coherence of both is guaranteed by the ultimate aesthetic and conceptual unity of the play itself (Stanislavsky defined this as the *superobjective*). The realistic criteria of consistency and coherence that we apply to dramatic characters are, properly speaking, properties of dramatic convention; they are not empirical or objective truths. Verisimilitude, none the less, assumes common-sense notions of what people are: unified, autonomous, 'free to choose'. The ideological dimension of this 'common sense' is something we shall return to below.

2 When Beatie arrives, the tone, pace and pattern of the dialogue, although still conversational, become more purposeful. Beatie, at least, seems to be interested in exchanging new ideas and information, challenging rather than simply confirming her mother's knowledge and beliefs. The dialogue between Beatie and Mrs Bryant subtly contrasts with the chat preceding it: there is an intensity and conviction (at least on her side) previously lacking. She uses language itself to rupture the boundaries of the Bryants'

linguistic, social and psychological universe; rather than reiterating well-worn and second-hand information and opinions, she is attempting to discover and express her authentic self through words (ironically, mainly by quoting the absent Ronnie). Given that her character development constitutes the dramatic interest and narrative dynamic of the play, her language moves the action significantly forward in a way that the phatic discourse of the others does not. For much of their conversation, Mrs Bryant and Beatie are at varying degrees of cross-purposes. It has a recurrent pattern. At every point that Beatie attempts to introduce subjects or opinions that are alien to the conversational and conceptual parameters of her mother's world, Mrs Bryant consciously or unconsciously parries with gossip. Dramatic conflict arises when Beatie's attempts to confront her mother with the emptiness and banality of her own discourse (and, by extension, of her whole existence) are sabotaged by Mrs Bryant's refusal to engage at the same conversational level.

The mobility and variety of Beatie's linguistic register are a major factor in the creation of the impression of awareness, self-consciousness and sensitivity. We might also note that the dichotomy that the play sustains between gossip and 'real' speech is implicitly gendered: conventionally, the aimlessness and inconsequentiality of the former is feminine, the purposeful and instrumental quality of the latter masculine. Perhaps Beatie acquires heroic status by learning to talk like a man.

In narrative terms, the illusion of independent life is sustained by an organic synthesis of plot and character, so that individual decisions and actions are seen as the source of action and meaning. Beatie's striving for self-determination through self-awareness is a central preoccupation of the bourgeois illusionist theatre; the Naturalistic hero's quest for freedom through self-knowledge is frequently the focus of empathy and identification for the spectator. This is itself a political emphasis: it connects with the bourgeois ideology of the individual and her or his 'voluntary' participation in the capitalist system. In this respect, we may well wonder at the moral that *Roots* offers: for an ostensibly socialist play, Beatie's achievement of triumphant individualism ('on my own two feet', p. 148) is at the expense of any social solution. It endorses a vision of self-improvement that in another context might appear suspiciously conservative.

3 Consciously or not, most characters in the play repeatedly draw attention to the action of speaking, to speech itself. This is partly the dialect, but there is a second layer of meaning. The limits and

possibilities of verbal communication are major concerns of the play; and there seems to be a direct connection with the limitations imposed upon individual freedom of action and expression.

Language itself may thus be seen as having an ideological as well as a dramatic significance. Speech and language are often the subject of the dialogue: characters comment upon the speech patterns of others (Ronnie and Beatie in particular); feuds are conducted by 'not speaking'; recurrent phrases are 'I'm telling you', or 'what are you saying'; and, of course, there are Beatie's persistent exhortations to her family to talk to her and to each other. The dialogue is marked by self-reflexivity, or in linguistic terms, *metalanguage*: talk about talk is a structural component of it. I would suggest that this conception of language is, like the notion of character, thoroughly implicated within ideology.

It is possible to read Beatie's attempts to transcend the limitations of the language community which she unwillingly inhabits as another aspect of the play's individualism: there is a sense that the 'banal' language used by the Beales and the Bryants is devalued by virtue of being 'common property'. Desiring unique and original self-expression, Beatie asserts her autonomy and independence, attempting (like Humpty Dumpty in *Alice Through the Looking Glass*) to master words rather than be mastered by them. 'Self-expression', the objective pursued by Beatie and the play, is a key concept, implying command of both self and speech, and emotional and intellectual presence in the act of speech itself. Freedom thus lies in the plenitude of articulacy. Ideology is at work here, in the assumption that individual consciousness may become somehow independent of language, indeed in command of it. This idea is conveyed explicitly through the metaphor of the bridge, as reported by Beatie (p. 90):

> Do you know what language is? Well, I'd never thought before – hev you? – it's automatic to you, isn't it, like walking? 'Well, language is words,' he'd say, as though telling me a secret. 'It's bridges, so that you can get safely from one place to another. And the more bridges you know about the more places you can see!'

The metalinguistic structure of this is complex: Beatie recounts Ronnie addressing her as an oracular authority on the subject of language. Speech, and hence thought, are essentially instrumental, to be manipulated by the self – the unproblematic 'you' happily traversing the bridge of articulacy. The image is in many ways an empowering one. For many oppressed groups, the struggle to find a voice is an essential first stage in asserting an identity; and the spoken and written words can be powerful weapons of liberation, as, for example, feminist critiques of the patriarchal bias of existing discourse have shown. But if the command of language may support the transformation from passive victim to active agent, this freedom has its limits. Post-structuralist linguistic theory, in particular, challenges the humanist account of the relationship between language and subjectivity. The post-structuralist would argue that consciousness does not exist prior to and beyond discourse, but is actually produced within it: 'it is language which enables the speaker to posit himself or herself as "I", as the subject of a sentence'.[3] Language thus affords the only terms within which consciousness is able to exist and operate; selfhood is not private but social. If we refer to Brecht's distinctions between the Dramatic and the Epic Theatre, we can see that these differing accounts of language embody the dichotomy between thought determining being and social being determining thought. The issue is more than a concept of language: it is to do with the nature and limits of individual freedom and agency. If Beatie learns to speak for herself by the end of the play, standing on her own two feet, where does she go from there?

II

In this and the next section we shall be looking at how a materialist understanding of subjectivity and the relationship between the self and the social process is reflected in the formal techniques used by Arden and Bond. In both plays it is probably less appropriate to think in terms of characterization than of the presentation of social roles. We shall first consider *Lear*, then *Serjeant Musgrave's Dance*.

Let us begin by again focusing upon language. In the Naturalist drama the structure of what is spoken implies the unspoken subtext, and this constitutes the emotional truth, depth and complexity of the character. This subjective presence is intuited through the actor identifying emotionally with, and the spectators projecting their own sense of self on to, the character (the subtext is not actually 'there'; it has to be *read into* the text). The relationship is one of *empathy*, a fusion of actor, role and spectator in the theatrical event, sustaining the reality of the dramatic fiction. The Epic Theatre constructs a more contradictory and critical relationship. **Would you now please give a close reading to Act 1, Scene 7 of *Lear* (in particular to the relationship between the Wife and the Boy) and consider the following questions:**

1 How would you describe the style of writing in this scene?
   What does it suggest about the 'inner life' of the speakers?
2 How important are empathy and identification here?
3 What relation does the dialogue have to the visual stagecraft of
   the scene? What does this suggest about how the roles are
   to be performed?

The following passages of commentary may be useful. The first is
from an account of rehearsals for a production of Brecht's *The
Caucasian Chalk Circle* by William Gaskill, who subsequently
directed many of Bond's plays at the Royal Court. The second is
from Bond's notes on the acting of his 1978 play *The Woman*:

> I was faced with the problem of how to start rehearsing, if you like,
> the Brechtian method as opposed to the Stanislavski method. So I
> started with a quite simple example. I asked the company for a
> cigarette. I said 'I'm out of cigarettes, I want a cigarette.' And one of
> the actresses, Mavis Edwards, gave me one. Then I asked, 'Why was
> I given this cigarette?' and the actors all gave reasons. One of the
> first was, 'Mavis is a generous person', and someone else said, 'No,
> she's not. You are the producer, and she's trying to get on your good
> side'. This went on, with various other suggestions, the interesting
> thing being that the first twenty or so answers were all based on
> emotional or psychological reasoning, involving the generosity of
> the actress and so on. The first, in fact the only, thing that went
> through the actors' minds was that it must be personally motivated.
> Eventually I got them to understand that this was only their way of
> looking at action in the theatre, that they automatically put an
> emotional stress on it. We discussed this ... and eventually they
> agreed that the giving of the cigarette was really quite a usual,
> habitual social action, that because we were director and an actress
> working together, there was nothing extraordinary in my asking for,
> or her giving of, a cigarette. I then pointed out that if we were to
> play this scene, and conveyed only the impression of generosity by
> the actress or of scrounging by me, we would not be truthful:
> because the giving of the cigarette was simply a social action, involv-
> ing little or no emotion.[4]

> We can think of a play as a story. The actors then become the
> illustrations of the story as well as the speakers of the text. When
> you are on the stage you should have a graphic sense. Use your
> acting as illustration. The artist emphasises the salient features. So
> must the actor. Don't let the emotion dictate the gesture ... our
> acting does not recreate. It recollects. Its energy is intellectual. It
> makes the particular general and the general particular. It finds the
> law in the incidental. Thus it restores moral importance to human
> behaviour.[5]

DISCUSSION

Compared with *Roots*, the dialogue appears rather sparse: direct, tersely informative rather than suggestive. If we read the dialogue for clues about character, we get a general impression of restrained antagonism and defensiveness. The language, however, does not draw the spectator in to the character in the way that Wesker's does: there is little basis for emotional identification. It seems to invite a more objective and detached response. The dialogue is constructed around specific, concrete images, which are integrated with the physical action of the scene.

One of the problems that we have to confront when reading or viewing a non-Naturalistic play is our own, largely unconscious, framework of expectations about the relationship between speech, subjectivity and character. The tenacity of these assumptions is illustrated by the constant temptation to interpret dramatic dialogue as individually expressive (Stanislavsky's notion of subtext is often regarded as a universal truth rather than a strategy of realism). The responses of Gaskill's actors, trained in the Stanislavskian techniques, may correspond to our first reading of Bond's text. Because there are elements of realism in the dialogue (that is, stylization is not visible in the form of obvious rhymes, rhythm, and so on), we may be led to speculate about the emotional lives of the speakers, their motives, thoughts and feelings. What do we make, for example, of the triangular relationship between the Boy, Cordelia and the Carpenter? Why does the Boy want to shelter Lear, and Cordelia want to get rid of him? What are Lear's feelings about staying with this family? In a realist text these would be immediate and pertinent questions, and the answers to them would create the subtext which establishes motivation and emotional truth. Most suggestively, silence, simplicity and brevity are often assumed to be highly charged with unspoken emotion.

The problem is that the emotional density which is characteristic of the Naturalistic theatre would here be counter-productive, undermining the gestic clarity of the scene and of the dramatic narrative. Rather than squeezing out ambiguities and multiple ironies from the dialogue, we should look for directness and clarity; the precise economy of the language is its narrative dynamic. Motive and emotional content are geared to suit the purposes of a developing analysis: the technique is argument, not suggestion. Instead of inviting the spectator to empathize with complex subjectivities, Bond presents action, speech and emotion as precise social facts. This does not mean that Bond is abstracting from or simplifying reality in a reductive sense, or that the roles are two-dimensional; simply that the social rather than the private significance of action serves as the focus of dramatic interest. It calls for a style of acting which avoids the distractions of naturalistic characterization without resorting to caricature or stereotype; the key technique is the recognition of difference rather than identification.

Performing the play thus requires an essentially illustrative, storytelling technique on the part of the actor, motivated by the *Gestus*, not the assumed subtext. The scene's central visual image, around which narrative, speech and action are organized, is the clothes-line hung with washing. The fact that domestic labour is not absorbed into the clutter of naturalistic mimesis focuses attention and charges the action with significance; by centring the scene on this image, Bond invites the spectator to read the dialogue and the action on a metaphoric as well as a realistic level. The dialogue is not distractingly hedged about with redundancy, hesitation or repetition: it is narrative rather than chat ('male' rather than 'female'?). The hanging of the sheets mirrors the building of the wall and recapitulates the central argument of the play: as Lear and Cordelia co-operate in this task their dialogue is riven by conflict. When Cordelia tells Lear of her desire to get rid of him, the line is between them – anticipating their confrontation in the penultimate scene, when he urges her to tear down the wall. The political meaning of this image is as important as the private feelings of the characters: the scene as a whole exemplifies Bond's illustrative technique.

I would like now to compare Bond's narrative and gestic method of writing for actors with Arden's technique. You will probably have noticed affinities between the two, particularly in the use of language and in the selective portrayal of behaviour. There is, however, a further sense in which acting roles in the Epic Theatre often confound the criteria of realism, that is, the common-sense conventions of consistent and appropriate behaviour and motive. Aiming to surprise the spectator, to de-familiarize human nature, the Epic Theatre, conversely, challenges the customary predictability and inevitability of action and emotion.

Reread Act 2, Scene 3, of *Serjeant Musgrave's Dance* in the light of the following critical comments:

> What I find absolutely unsatisfactory about these three soldiers is the way they react to Annie in the stable. The scene is conceived like a

ballad, with the girl offering herself to each of the men in turn ...
Hurst's and Attercliffe's rejection of Annie have nothing to do with
particular experience at all – it's a reaction imposed on them in
order to achieve an illustration of human experience in general.[6]

Arden, like Brecht, is interested in making us question the 'self-
evident', in making us see the everyday world with fresh eyes. This is
not a scene about individual feelings: rather it is what Brecht called a
Gestus, a whole complex of speech, acts, gestures and music which
denotes social relationships.[7]

**How does Arden combine ballad conventions with more realistic
techniques in the portrayal of Annie and the soldiers in this scene?
Is it a successful combination?**

DISCUSSION

The ballad elements I would identify as Sparky's song, the simple
and clear-cut expression of emotion by Annie and the three
soldiers, and the triadic structure of the action. The motives of
the three soldiers, however, are perhaps more 'realistically'
ambiguous and contradictory.

We have seen in Chapter 3 that Arden invokes the technique
of the ballad as a model for the stylization of action, emotion and
situation that we see in the play as a whole. It is an appropriate
framework for this scene. The ballad's primary colours match the
directness and simplicity of the emotions, its symmetrical rhythm
and pattern the overall structure of the scene. The ballad tradition
also deals with the general rather than the particular, representative experience rather than that of the unique individual. Here,
we are concerned with the interaction between Annie and the
soldiers. This is initially framed by Sparky's song:

> She came to me at midnight
> With moonlight on her arms
> And I told her not to make no noise
> Nor cause no wild alarms.
> But her savage husband he awoke
> And up the stairs did climb
> To catch her in her very deed:
> So fell my fatal crime ...

Private emotion is less important here than the establishment of an
emblematic framework for the action. Annie goes to each of the
three soldiers, and, for different reasons, is twice rejected. Hurst
invokes Musgrave's 'word' as a source of strength which overrides
desire; Attercliffe points to the blood on his hands as corrupting

human and sexual contact; but Sparky offers to run away with
her. This precipitates the climax to the scene, the fight between
Sparky and Hurst, with Attercliffe attempting to intervene; which
switches from broad farce – the tug-of-war with Sparky's trousers
– to tragedy, as Sparky is (perhaps accidentally) stabbed to death.

The scene focuses attention not on the individual feelings of
the soldiers but upon conflicting attitudes towards the soldier's
duty. Hurst embodies an extreme of duty and loyalty, Sparky its
antithesis, with Attercliffe negotiating between them. Annie – the
female role – catalyses the conflict. The dialectic is between the
order of the word and the anarchy of desire; the strong visual
counterpoint to this is the brooding presence of Musgrave himself
upstage. The action and stagecraft are, like Bond's, illustrative,
inviting the spectator to read the scene as allegory: motivation is
subordinate to exposition. But the play is not *consistent* in its
use of the ballad form, and it is this that may make it seem
unsatisfactory. Desire cuts across the analysis of duty, and the
personal dimension is intermingled with the political. Thus it
confronts common-sense expectations concerning the behaviour of
'sex-starved' soldiers, and throws new light on the ballad pattern.
It is as if Arden sets up a conspicuously artificial structure of
action and motive in order to test its validity: the pattern does not
quite cohere. It prevents the actions of the soldiers from simply
being seen as a predictable narrative of male sexual aggression.
The soldiers do not behave in the ways predicted either by the
ballad structure or by conventional realism, but the confrontation
of the two discourses enforces a complex seeing which takes
account of both.

Throughout this section, I have avoided wherever possible the
terms 'character' and 'characterization' in my discussion of the
acting roles in *Lear* and *Serjeant Musgrave's Dance*. This is not
merely a technical point: the uncritical application of the concept
implies a universalization of its implicit ideologies of self and
human nature. Beatie Bryant's apotheosis is to become such a
character, presenting a confident and illusory image of herself
as an autonomous speaking subject – full of words which Ronnie
still owns. Brecht, Bond and Arden would contest this victory: the
subject of the Epic Theatre is, in Walter Benjamin's phrase, 'like
an empty stage on which the contradictions of our society are
acted out'.[8] But if the present disturbing reality is fragmentation,
Arden and Bond recognize that collective rather than individual
struggle may yet refashion the self as a more substantial – and
truly revolutionary – agent of historical change. As Mrs Hitchcock

reminds Musgrave at the end of *Serjeant Musgrave's Dance*, it was simple hunger that forced the colliers to reject his revolution. 'One day they'll be full, though, and the Dragoons'll be gone, and then they'll remember.'

5. Genre and Metadrama

In this chapter we will look at two aspects of the three plays which have already been touched upon in previous chapters: their sources and textual analogues; and dramatic and theatrical self-consciousness. The two aspects, as we shall see, are interconnected. We shall consider *Lear* first and then *Serjeant Musgrave's Dance* and *Roots*. Our discussion of the first play will be mainly in terms of its relationship with Shakespeare's *King Lear*.

I

Thus far we have treated *Lear* as more or less a play in its own right. In doing so, we have excluded from our analysis a vital constituent of its meaning and effect: its relationship with Shakespeare's *King Lear*. What this relationship is, how it is manifested, and the significance it has are the concerns of this section. A working knowledge of Shakespeare's play is necessary for this discussion; if you have not read it in its entirety, then please read the following scenes: Act 1, Scene 1; Act 1, Scene 4; Act 2, Scene 4; Act 3, Scene 8; Act 4, Scene 6; Act 4, Scene 7; Act 5, Scene 3.

We will begin with the broad similarities and divergences between the two in terms of plot, structure and character. **How does Bond rework Shakespeare's material? What are the most important differences and similarities between the two plays?**

DISCUSSION

Both plays show a ruler who is initially arbitrary and despotic, who is rejected by his amoral and violent daughters, and who goes mad. The recovery of his sanity brings with it insight into the realities of social injustice and inhumanity. Both plays dramatize this in terms of the upheaval of an entire society through civil war. The most significant differences I would cite are in the refusal of tragedy in Bond's play, and in the portrayal of Cordelia.

The broad similarities in terms of the scope, scale and course of the action are clear enough. Continuity is found in the use of analogous roles: apart from Lear, we have Cordelia (no longer Lear's daughter, however), Bodice and Fontanelle (Regan and Goneril) and the Gravedigger's Boy (a composite of Edgar, the Fool and Kent). Some of the incidents and situations are similar: Warrington's torture and deafening at the hands of Bodice and Fontanelle corresponds to Gloucester's blinding, which is transferred to Lear himself; while Lear's trial (Act 2, Scene 1) parallels the mock-trial in Shakespeare (Act 3, Scene 6); Lear's pastoral interlude with the Gravedigger's Boy (Bond) evokes King Lear's experiences on the heath (Shakespeare); and so on. There is a continuity of imagery and metaphor, particularly in the relation of human and natural worlds, and in the exploration of both blindness and madness. Moreover, the plays have similarities in terms of setting: the anachronisms of Bond's play parallel Shakespeare's own mixture of Renaissance, feudal and pagan elements in the world of *King Lear*.[1]

On the whole, these points of contact heighten the differences between the two plays, not only in events but also in their implications, and in the moral and political conclusions that can be drawn from each. The world of Bond's play is in every sense a more pitiless and brutal one than that of Shakespeare's. I mean this not only in terms of its proportionately greater emphasis upon, and graphic quality of, physical violence but also in its rigorously unsentimental analysis of power politics. Bond's Lear has no intention of relinquishing his authority. The civil war is the consequence of his concerted efforts to *consolidate* his power. Already we can see the divergence between Shakespeare's view and Bond's: for the former, violence and disorder spring from the abdication or usurpation of authority, whereas for the latter they result from authority itself. Bond places less emphasis than Shakespeare on the father–daughter relationship: from the outset Lear sees Bodice and Fontanelle primarily as political opponents. Bond does not deal with 'filial ingratitude', which is the recurrent preoccupation of Shakespeare's play, and a focus for empathy with King Lear. Neither is there a polarization of morally and politically 'good' and sympathetic roles and evil ones, as in Shakespeare. Bond's Lear, and subsequently Cordelia, is equally as ruthless as Bodice and Fontanelle. Bond also indicates, in the first prison scene (Act 2, Scene 2) how the daughters' behaviour and identity have been shaped by Lear himself and the power structures he has perpetuated. In Bond's play, evil – if the term has any meaning at all – is a social rather than a metaphysical force. Shakespeare, nevertheless, offers the possibility of catharsis and ultimate reassurance by allowing goodness a measure of triumph over evil in the restitution, however tentative, of order at the end of the play. Bond ends with Lear's sudden death.

Bond's refusal of the sentimentality that has been projected onto Shakespeare's play is most clearly demonstrated in his treatment of Cordelia. His reworking of this role is in fact a crucial element in the relationship between the two plays, and it most effectively illustrates the gap between them. We shall therefore now be concerned with the main points of contact between the two Cordelias.

1 Concentrating mainly upon *actions*, make notes on what seem to you to be the most important points of similarity and difference between Bond's and Shakespeare's portrayals of Cordelia. What effect do Bond's shifts of emphasis have on our response to the role, and on her role in the play as a whole? You should bear in mind Bond's view of Shakespeare's Cordelia:

One of the very important things in the play was to re-define the relationship between Cordelia and Lear. I don't want to make this seem easy or slick, but Cordelia in Shakespeare's play is an absolute menace. I mean, she's a very dangerous type of person, and I thought that the other daughters, though I'm not excusing them, were very unfairly treated and misunderstood.[2]

2 Compare Act 5, Scene 2, of *King Lear* with Act 3, Scenes 4 and 5 of *Lear*, focusing in particular upon the relationships between Lear and Cordelia, and Lear and the Gravedigger's Boy. How do the scenes connect with each other? In what ways does Bond's treatment offer a commentary upon Shakespeare's?

DISCUSSION

1 The immediate difference between the two is that Bond transforms Cordelia from an essentially passive to an active figure. There has been a strong tradition in the critical and theatrical history of Shakespeare's play to sentimentalize and idealize Cordelia; largely, I suspect, because (unlike the other women in the play) she appeals to male critical sensibilities by suffering in silence (as King Lear comments after her death (Act 5, Scene 3, l. 270), 'Her voice was ever soft, /Gentle and and low – an excellent thing in a woman'). Her actions are all geared towards acquiescence – even her initial refusal to participate in the love-test springs from a deeper love and duty – and obedience; and her unquestioning loyalty and forgiveness simply intensify as the play goes on. This is naturalized by the familial relationship: the play demands that we see Cordelia in subordinate relation to Lear, the focus throughout – and particularly in the final scenes – is on the father–daughter 'bond'. The ethic of love and generosity that Cordelia embodies is a source of optimism, of possible redemption, in the otherwise pitiless world of the play.

Bond's rewriting of the role of Cordelia stresses agency rather than passivity, but he is careful not simply to reverse the terms so that she emerges as villainous rather than heroic. Whereas in *King Lear* Cordelia's 'goodness', like her sisters' evil, is a given quality, Bond shows actions, and their moral implications and consequences, rooted in social causes; in the process he foregrounds some of the awkward questions and contradictions that are latent in Shakespeare's text. Shakespeare's play glosses over the realities of Cordelia's war against her sisters – force, not abstract goodness, determines the outcome of the play. There is a disparity between Cordelia's personal virtue and her political role; the contradiction becomes apparent in her defeat. In Bond's play this aspect is developed: Cordelia's revolution perpetuates oppression because it reproduces the violent tactics of those it sought to overthrow. In the final analysis, the idealization of Cordelia in Shakespeare's play is an endorsement, not a critique, of traditional authority.

2 The effects of the final scenes of the two plays are very different. The main differences are that Bond stresses confrontation rather than personal reconciliation, and that he ends with an image of public political action rather than private grief. Comparing them, we can bring together the various strands of our discussion. We see a starkly contrasting pattern of relationships. In *King Lear* the scene begins with an emblem of reconciliation as King Lear and

Cordelia are led off to prison; it ends with an archetypal image of loss which is none the less an affirmation of the personal bond: the father dying over the body of his daughter. *Lear* evokes that pattern, but rearranges its constituent elements in order to produce a radically different effect. Lear's confrontation with Cordelia provokes him to attack the wall in the final scene. In Shakespeare's play, the audience is emotionally compelled to empathize with King Lear's terminal anguish. In Bond's, we observe the progression from rational decision to action. The role of the Ghost in the scene is pivotal. Up to the penultimate scene he has fulfilled in personal and emotional terms the role that Cordelia has for Lear in Shakespeare's play. At great emotional cost, Lear rejects the empathy that the Ghost demands, to move beyond the personal solutions he offers to positive political action. The image of the Ghost in Lear's arms invokes King Lear with Cordelia; except that Lear wills the Ghost to *die*. The death of the Ghost is separated from that of Lear by the scene break. Bond does not fuse them together in an emotional climax: the audience is left to think about Lear's action, rather than his feelings.

This conclusion offers a sharp and critical contrast to the ending of Shakespeare's play. *King Lear* takes its hero to a point of recognition but emphasizes his ultimate powerlessness; the tragic moral is that the appalling sufferings shown in the play are unavoidable. King Lear's moral and personal transformation is the discovery of empathy; through the recognition of personal vulnerability he arrives at an awareness of common humanity and of the fallibility of human justice. But he (and Shakespeare, perhaps) cannot progress beyond this insight, and indeed in the final scenes he actually attempts to escape from the public world into a private realm, into a sentimental idyll with Cordelia. In Bond's play it is the Ghost who wants to retreat from reality, responsibility and the possibility of action. Lear rejects this; and in so doing he moves beyond tragedy, towards revolution.

I would like now briefly to consider some of the implications that this has for *Lear* in formal terms. A major effect of the presence of *King Lear* as a co-text, I would suggest, is that it makes *Lear* itself to a certain extent self-reflexive or metadramatic: that is, Bond's play incorporates within itself an awareness of its own theatrical and textual status.

The intertextual relation between the two plays creates a double perspective: the world of *Lear* simultaneously is and is not a self-contained dramatic fiction (complex seeing again). Viewed alongside *King Lear*, Bond's play precipitates rupture and dislocation, with incidents and characters from Shakespeare

conflated, inverted or distorted – contributing to the anachron-
istic nightmare-reality effect (discussed in Chapter 3). The
Shakespearian echoes haunt the play: Lear's actions are illumi-
nated and contextualized by our knowledge of what happens to
King Lear. In itself this is an alienation effect, and this sense of
alternative possibilities was, for Brecht, an important aspect of the
Epic Theatre: 'People ought never to be treated as if they can only
act one way; they could act differently. Our houses have fallen
about our ears; they could be standing.'[3] Our ghostly appre-
hension of Shakespeare's play is brought into sharp focus at key
moments. A powerful example of this occurs in Act 1, Scene 7,
when the Gravedigger's Boy cries 'Cordelia!' as he is shot: the
evocation of Shakespearian 'goodness' acts here almost as a
desperate prayer. Act 2, Scene 6, which includes both the autopsy
and the blinding of Lear, is particularly dense with allusions and
echoes. I would like you to consider two key passages in Bond,
and their counterparts in Shakespeare:

1 Reread the autopsy sequence (pp. 58–60) in the light of *King
   Lear*, Act 3, Scene 6, l. 74:

   King Lear: Let them anatomize Regan, see what breeds about her
   heart. Is there any cause in nature that make these hard hearts?

   How does Shakespeare's metaphor contribute to the meaning of
   the scene? Does Bond suggest an answer to the question?
2 Compare the blinding of Lear (pp. 63–4) with the blinding of
   Gloucester (*King Lear*, Act 3, Scene 7). What do you make of
   the differences in tone, and in the depiction of violence?

DISCUSSION

The implicit reference to Shakespeare's metaphor draws together a
central concern of both plays, which is presented and explored in
different ways: the origins of human evil. The key phrase in
Bond's text is 'this isn't an instrument of torture, but a scientific
device'. Gloucester's blinding is overwhelmingly emotional
in impact, as sadistic impulses compound the punishment for
treachery (i.e. helping King Lear escape). Lear's blinding is
intended to render him politically ineffective by sending him
insane; it has a grotesque rationality about it.
    Shakespeare offers no reply to King Lear's question as to
whether the cruelty of the daughters has a cause in nature: the
lack of resolution exposes an ideological blind-spot in the discourse of the play. By theatricalizing the metaphor, Bond exposes

the belief in inherent human evil and brutality as ideological; anatomizing Regan/Fontanelle, he forces the point that the wickedness of 'hard hearts' is the product not of God nor of nature but of social injustice; moreover, that Lear himself, as a representative of a brutal and brutalizing power system, has a responsibility for what has happened (an implication which Shakespeare evades). It is a vital point, and it is imperative that its theatrical impact should not overwhelm the metaphoric and political significance.

For the scene to work on this level (and not only as Grand Guignol), the spectator needs to be aware of the structure of textual meaning within which it operates. Invoking Shakespeare's text at this point is a means of cushioning the impact of the moment by transferring it to the level of metaphor – the added dimension to the aggro-effect that invites the spectator to respond intellectually as well as emotionally. This applies also to the blinding sequence. First, the physical horror is intensified because it is enacted upon Lear himself. In Shakespeare's text there is a hierarchy of suffering, in the sense that King Lear, being of greater social, and hence tragic, stature than Gloucester, does not experience pain inflicted upon the body to anything like the same degree. Although critical and theatrical tradition has maintained that this ensures that Lear's tragedy is consequently the more profound, it also makes it easier to idealize in Christian or humanist terms; and it is, ultimately, more reassuring. Mental suffering can be tolerated by audiences, being regarded as somehow mystically purgative and regenerative, rather more readily than can physical torture. As a materialist, Bond repudiates the dualism of mind and body that allows the illusion of transcendence, the utopian flight from reality that is King Lear's preferred solution at the end of the play. Confronting the spectator with the graphic depiction of disfigurement, Bond locates the fragmentation of the self in the body of the actor, and in the real time and space of performance. It is in every sense a painful process.

The texts diverge on the motivation for the blinding and on how it is carried out. Shakespeare emphasizes the barbarism of the perpetrators, and the incident signals the collapse of order, morality and humanity into chaos and savagery. Bond, on the other hand, stresses the efficiency and the clinical objectivity of the operation: the Fourth Prisoner simply carries out a task deemed politically necessary. The grotesque aspect is emphasized by the utilitarianism, as the 'vile jelly' is extracted undamaged and 'put to good use'. The 'soothing solution of formaldehyde crystals' and the aerosol are the counterparts of the flax and egg whites provided by Cornwall's servants. The effect is alienatory, and critical of Shakespeare's text: the Fourth Prisoner's humane damage limitation interrogates Shakespeare's faith in the capacity of individual acts of charity to ameliorate the systematic brutality of the state.

II

Lear draws considerable significance from the audience's knowledge of a co-text. The other two plays we are studying do not appear, on the surface, to exhibit any similar close relationship with a dramatic source; in this respect they are less overtly 'self-conscious'. The existence of multiple referential and fictive layers in *Lear* problematizes its own representation, and the process by which the audience assimilates meaning is a complex one: instead of unconsciously accepting the truth and reality of the representation (as in the illusionist theatre) it has to negotiate an interplay between fiction, metafiction and reality. Both *Serjeant Musgrave's Dance* and *Roots* seem to present an altogether more direct and less problematic correspondence between dramatic fiction and reality, in the sense that both can be seen as (with varying degrees of stylization) reflecting or reproducing a recognizable and authentic 'real world'. In this section I wish to examine how far this is true by a brief discussion of both plays.

We have already discussed some of the metadramatic elements used in *Serjeant Musgrave's Dance*, in particular the relationship between the audience and the stage, in Chapter 3. What I aim to explore here are the ways in which the audience's overall response to the play is shaped by, and mediated through, its awareness of dramatic and theatrical convention, that is, how the play works upon the *expectations* of the audience. We can begin by identifying what some of those expectations are, by identifying some of the dramatic discourses that Arden draws upon.

The ballad-like aspect of the form and structure has already been noted: the clear-cut patterns of behaviour and narrative, the stark antitheses and sharp contrasts, the regularity and symmetry of the action. Its material is elemental and archetypal conflict; its essence is the stock situation; it has a recognizable predictability of structure, action and character. A second model is the medieval Morality play, which perhaps lies behind Arden's definition of the play as an 'unhistorical parable'. Like the ballad, the Morality play employs stark antitheses. Its dramatic agents are not char-

acters but representative figures and personifications of ideas and
values: Good Deeds, Lust, Everyman. Unlike the ballad, where,
according to Arden, 'we are given the fable, and we draw our own
conclusions',[4] the Morality play is didactic, in that it dramatizes
dogma. Thus we might see *Serjeant Musgrave's Dance* as being
peopled by figures who are essentially personified ideas: Musgrave
as Duty, the Bargee as Self-interest, and so on. There is also
a medieval element in the play's central emblem of Musgrave
dancing under the shadow of the skeleton on the scaffold, re-
calling the iconography of the Dance of Death.

A third model is the Victorian melodrama, which the play
evokes in both setting and situation. As Katherine Worth points
out:

> It was from the annals of crime as they were recorded in such places
> as the 'sensation' ballads that the characteristic plots of these melo-
> dramas were drawn. And it was toward a grim final scene of
> social vengeance that the action often flowed.[5]

Worth cites the gallows as a recurrent motif in melodrama which
also forms the figurative centre of *Serjeant Musgrave's Dance*.
Again, the schematic dramatic and moral world of melodrama,
with its villainous employers, Mayor and Constable, provides a
possible framework for Arden's play.

A fourth model was suggested by Arden himself in an interview, when he stated that one of the sources for the play was a
Hollywood Western directed by Hugo Fregonese, *The Raid*:

> A group of men – Confederate soldiers in disguise – ride into a
> Northern town. Three quarters of the film is taken up with their
> installation in the town, and the various personal relationships they
> establish. On the appointed morning, they all turn out in their
> Confederate uniforms, hoist a flag in the square, rob a bank and
> burn the houses. Finally . . . the cavalry arrives at the last minute,
> although in this case they are too late.[6]

These are only four possible models for the play. There are a
number of other literary, dramatic and artistic traditions which it
can be seen to draw upon: I have suggested the influence of the
pantomime tradition in the play's stagecraft, but there are also
English folk and mummers' plays, and, at the visual level, the
paintings of L.S. Lowry. The question is whether these hetero-
geneous discourses can be said to cohere as a unified whole.
**Although there are clear continuities between some of these
traditions, are there not equally clear contradictions between
them? Does the attempt to combine the ballad and the parable
form result in confusion because the frameworks of expectations**

constructed by the individual conventions are incompatible with each other?

DISCUSSION

Once again, it would seem, contradiction is the key to the play's effect. By combining elements of various traditions, Arden arouses expectations in order to contradict and frustrate them; the audience is expected continually to redefine and rethink its response. The disparity between these elements is Arden's method of representing and analysing the complexity of the political and moral contradictions that the play deals with. There is a general point to be drawn from this. If the ambivalence of response that *Serjeant Musgrave's Dance* generates is grounded in its problematic and ambiguous relationship with conventional dramatic and theatrical expectations, then this intertextual element might be seen as characteristic of *all* dramatic texts. We evaluate the meaning and effect of a dramatic text not through a simple one-to-one correspondence with reality but through the permutations and transformations it enacts upon established dramatic and theatrical conventions: in this respect all texts are, in a general sense, self-reflexive. This is true even of realist texts, where the chief aim is, apparently, to conceal the text's own artifice. We can see this happening in *Roots*. As we have seen in Chapters 3 and 4, the integrity and authenticity of Naturalistic illusion are evaluated *vis-à-vis* existing dramatic conventions. Consider these reviewers' comments upon the first production of the play:

> John Dexter, the director, has been extremely daring in his use of slowness and silence. Accustomed to the slickness and speed, we may find it difficult to accept this pace at first; but he insists from the start and soon takes us with him. Ponderous slowness, pointless reiteration, stubborn taciturnity, cowlike vacuity – I have never seen these so perfectly caught on the stage. But the fact that they manage to be neither boring nor depressing is the highest tribute I can pay to Mr Dexter and his admirable cast.[7]

> ... exactly the kind of thing Shaftesbury Avenue never finds room for. It is original, entertaining, with a hard core of social criticism, well produced and acted admirably by the Coventry company. It might easily have been Cold Comfort: it is in fact rural kitchen sink.[8]

> Taken separately, the details he accumulates are frequently comic; his achievement is to have set them in a context of such tangible reality that sympathy banishes belly-laughs. It is Chekhov's method, applied not to the country gentry but to the peasants at the gate.[9]

As the first passage indicates, the realistic effect is at least partly due to the way in which the play flouts conventional dramatic expectations. But we may extend this analysis on to a structural level, in the sense that we can see it as a technique which is part of the play's political project. Notice that in order to describe and evaluate Wesker's Naturalistic method, two of these reviewers not only invoke explicit literary and dramatic models, but that this centres on the representation of *class*. The third passage, in particular, implies a reversal of expectations in the method of representation: the 'peasants' have moved from the periphery to the centre of the drama.

We can see this inversion of the conventional dramatic and class hierarchy particularly clearly in the episode of the appearance of Mr Healey in Act 2 (pp. 118–19). What do you make of Healey as a character? How would you relate this to his class position?

DISCUSSION

Healey is clearly a minor character: he is defined in a few words, and his role seems purely functional, even stereotyped. This is his only appearance in the play, and we are not supplied with any more than the bare minimum of information about the character apart from 'a firm, not unkind, but business-is-business voice' (speech again) with 'that apologetic threat even in his politeness'. The characterization is purely functional. He is, simply, the farm manager, and his dramatic function is twofold: to prepare the audience for the cutting of Mr Bryant's wages, and to convey the news of Stan Mann's death. In this respect, Healey fulfils the classic messenger function of the walk-on part.

Here, I would suggest, is a subtle yet significant shift of dramatic perspective. Note the class element: Healey is a bourgeois and an employer, but relegated to a theatrically subordinate role. This is the *formal* aspect of Wesker's sympathetic and 'authentic' portrayal of working-class and rural life, a confrontation of conventional expectations as to *who* is considered dramatically interesting, who should be the protagonist of the drama. In this Wesker is reacting against the dominant bourgeois tradition in English drama, wherein, typically, the working class appears in a servile (or menacing) capacity, in sentimentalized, patronizing or grotesquely caricatured forms: as drunken servants, comic gardeners, and prostitutes with hearts of gold. We might see the play as reversing these terms of dramatic representation; an interrogation of its conventional class perspective. But there is a sting in the tail. Healey impinges upon the action to an extent markedly disproportionate to his visibility as a character, when later in the play we learn that he has cut Mr Bryant's hours. It is still evident where the real power lies. Looking at the employer–employee relationship from an unconventional angle, we are invited to share the perspective of the exploited; in its own way it is an alienation effect.

We will now look at another cultural discourse operative in the play. This is the literary and cultural tradition of the *pastoral*, a mode of representation which frequently involves a nostalgic and romantic idealization of 'natural' rural life. Central to the pastoral ideal is a moral as well as a geographical polarization between the city and the country, between urban and rural existence. Raymond Williams offers a succinct formulation of this dichotomy:

> On the country has gathered the idea of a natural way of life: of peace, innocence, and simple virtue. On the city has gathered the idea of an achieved centre: of learning, communication, light. Powerful hostile associations have also developed: on the city as a place of noise, worldliness and ambition; on the country as a place of backwardness, ignorance, limitation. A contrast between country and city, as fundamental ways of life, reaches back into classical times.[10]

Williams traces this binary opposition through the English literary tradition, arguing that the association of the country with a bucolic Golden Age acts as a potent myth. The city, the cradle of destructive and alienating industrialism, can be placed against a stable 'tradition' and natural order. But, as Williams points out, this idealization requires a systematic misrepresentation of the real conditions of rural social existence, in that its real property and labour relations must be disguised, suppressed or obliterated. The pastoral ideal is ideologically important because it offers a mythical resolution of the contradictions of capitalism, or at least a refuge from its excesses; in a sense it undermines the demand for revolutionary socialism (usually seen as a city-based movement). The illusory solution offered to Lear by the Gravedigger's Boy is pastoral: escape from the pressures of the present into private nostalgia.

With these ideas in mind, I would like you to consider their significance in relation to *Roots*. Look in particular at the presentation of work in the play, and at the significance throughout of the imagery of nature (in, for example, the play's title). Does the

play present a moral and political dichotomy between country and city along the lines described? How might you relate it to the pastoral tradition?

DISCUSSION

The picture of rural life presented in the play is hardly an idyllic or romantic one: the overall impression we form is of harsh, subsistence living; less obvious is the way in which this picture offers a developing analysis of the situation through a subtle manipulation and confrontation of pastoral conventions. The action is structured around work. The play begins with Jimmy's arrival home, followed by the argument between himself and Beatie over the bus strike, farm labourers' wages and the need for solidarity between urban and rural workers; Act 2 centres on Mr Bryant and his imminent demotion; while the women throughout are perpetually engaged in domestic labour. The argument between Jimmy and Beatie establishes very early on the essential continuity between city and country work (Jimmy is a garage mechanic): the characters are workers, subject to the same exploitative labour relations as their city counterparts (in fact, the abrupt cut in Mr Bryant's wages indicates a particularly naked form of capitalism). But the play also emphasizes that the most exploited groups of workers are often the most reactionary. Property relations are also suggested, significantly, through the medium of nature. The discussion of the conditions of farm labourers is underscored by Jimmy sharpening a reap hook (perhaps Wesker is playing with the iconography of the hammer and sickle here) as he prepares to go out and work on 'his' allotment. One of the main conflicts of Acts 1 and 2 centres on the refusal of Mr Bryant to allow 'his' electricity to be used. It seems that the shortage of amenities (one way of distinguishing rural from urban life) elicits less homespun virtue than petty competition.

The imagery of nature runs through the play, but the conventional pastoral meanings that accrue around it are subjected to some critical scrutiny. Rather than being simply innocent, virtuous, regenerative, 'the natural' is subjected to complex and conflicting appropriations. The title of the play is, of course, loaded with irony. Initially, we expect it to have a positive significance, as it suggests familial and historical tradition, a conservative celebration of permanence and continuity. The implication is that Beatie's return to her family and country origins will be a source of regeneration and development; it also suggests an organic richness and unity within the community itself. But the play undermines that idyllic view: the rural life to which Beatie returns is shown to be riven by conflict rather than unified, sterile rather than regenerative. Beatie's 'roots' are a stultifying, deadening force: we see her family (her mother in particular) actually stifling her growth and development. But there is a further, possibly contradictory, sense in which the term is used, one that is made explicit towards the end of the play, in the dialogue between Beatie and her family (pp. 145–6) which centres on her assertion that 'we've got no roots'.

In the light of the above discussion, how does this dialogue make use of the opposition between nature and culture? Do you see any contradiction in the metaphor that Beatie uses?

DISCUSSION

The imagery of 'roots' is, rather unexpectedly, used as a metaphor for *cultural* enrichment: the 'natural' state of rural and urban life is one of impoverishment. At first reading, the sense of what Beatie is saying is clear enough: 'rootlessness' designates the ignorance and spiritual and cultural impoverishment of herself and her class. The image of roots is used in the sense of intimate and meaningful connections between the self, society and history. Wesker is thus reorientating an image which is conventionally used to signify the transitory and fragmented, alienating nature of *urban* experience, the idea of being cut off from nature and the land (Beatie says: 'I ent got no roots – just like town people – just a mass o' nothin'.'). Wesker thus resists and interrogates elements of pastoral ideology; the personal regeneration that Beatie seeks is only attainable through political and cultural transformation, not through some rediscovery of organic natural unity or tradition. And yet, paradoxically, Beatie's polemic is implicated within the assumptions which it attacks. Although roots are invested elsewhere in the play with negative connotations, suggesting a stubborn conservatism, here they are claimed as a source of strength. This, in effect, supplants one idea of tradition with another – a utopianism which is still embedded in the past. We should also note that there is a subtle but significant difference between being rootless and having roots which are impoverished; and yet the two images are combined in the speech. Beatie claims that 'we've got no roots' while simultaneously declaring the need to keep their roots strong; the speech manages to elide the two senses. This is not a minor inconsistency, but one which points to a central paradox in the play's argument about culture and character. Wesker is attempting to argue for the development of an organic wholeness of personality through the acquisition of culture as a fundamentally natural process; but his essentialist faith that it is the inner resources of character that ultimately produce autonomous and unified subjectivity introduces an alternative, and conflicting, conception of the 'natural self'. This conflict is embodied in the contradictory imagery of the play's title.

The reiteration of the play's title is an implicitly metadramatic device. Does this signal to the spectator that here is the 'meaning' or 'message' of the play? The location of the speech at the moment of crisis and of personal revelation seems to imply a compellingly 'authoritative' disclosure of meaning. It is a continuation of the device of attributing cultural and political commentary to the absent Ronnie, but it is here divested of the – both literal and metaphorical – quotation marks that tended to frame, distance and ironize Ronnie's views. But if, like me, you remain unconvinced by the means that Wesker uses to attempt to reconcile a political analysis of working-class culture with the requirements of Naturalistic illusion, you may also feel that the emphatic espousal of a message disrupts the consistency of character, dialogue and situation. Isn't Beatie's sudden articulacy more a pretext for breaking the constraints of Naturalistic illusion?

We might see this sudden collapse of verisimilitude as a contradiction within the form itself, or more precisely between form and political content. I would suggest (and this is a consciously 'perverse' interpretation – a Brechtian strategy, if you like) that *Roots* struggles to contain, within the framework of realism, a political and dramatic self-consciousness which ultimately disrupts its formal unity. The impersonation of Ronnie, a performance within a performance, is one such device, offering a critical perspective upon the 'reality' within which it is ostensibly contained.

The most intriguing use of metadrama, however, is in Act 3, when Beatie – having made her mother play the role of judge – presents her family with a moral conundrum (pp. 139–40). **Would you now reread this passage, and consider the following questions:**

What metadramatic significance might this have? How might this affect the role of empathy and identification in the audience's response to the play and to Beatie?

DISCUSSION

The problem seems to operate on two levels: within the fiction of the play, and as a commentary upon it. Read within the Naturalistic framework of the play, Beatie's aim is to 'get you buggers thinking if it's the last thing I do'. She is only partially successful: Pearl and Frank show a degree of engagement with the problem, but Mrs Bryant, Jenny and Jimmy reject it out of hand. In realistic terms, the incident simply continues the exposition of Beatie's relationship with her family. But 'you buggers' might include the off-stage as well as the on-stage audience: the problem is also presented to us. The irony is that the girl's situation clearly parallels Beatie's own. We might interpret the passage as a sort of synopsis of the main action. But there are other implications. The parallel with Beatie's situation also provides a neat way of framing not only it but the play as a whole: by using a story to set a moral problem Wesker reminds us both of the fictional nature of the larger story within which it is contained, and of its moral and ethical implications. We are invited to suspend our belief in the illusion and consider it, momentarily, in the terms of a moral problem; that is, to appraise the action critically and intellectually rather than surrender to empathy. Interestingly, not only is it a problem without an immediately clear or definitive solution; it is also one which bears an ambiguous relation to the play itself. With whom is Ronnie to be identified? Archie or Tom? The other effect is that by inviting a critical, thoughtful appraisal of this problem, the text prepares a possible response to Beatie's rejection: in this sense it is alienatory. In the same way that Beatie asks her audience not to empathize with the girl but to evaluate the situation, the text momentarily suspends empathy and invites the audience to think and to judge. It is one of the key moments in the play; and in that it begins to subvert the play's commitment to the principles of illusionism, it may be where its genuinely radical potential lies. If pressed, *Roots* may be more open to the play of contradictions than it first appears.

6. Theatres and Audiences

Who are our audience?
We write for those who carry bricks
Not for those who hire the builders
The hirer's world is a dream
It floats on a painted cloud
The hirer may sit in our audience
We speak to him
But he is an onlooker
Only the others can judge
The hirer reverses all human standards
And all human values
We write for those he exploits
If we give them a key
They know if the key will open the door
They built the door
It is as simple as that.[1]

Throughout this guide we have focused upon the theatrical potential of our three plays. Because in practice this quality reaches outside the text into the public theatrical arena where it is performed, fuller discussion will move from the words on the page to their conditions of articulation in performance. To assess the social significance of any drama we need to see it in the context of the theatre within which it originates, and in relation to the audience for whom it is performed.

In this chapter I wish to reintroduce some of the specific theatrical and institutional contexts that have been central to the production and reproduction of our three plays – focusing in particular upon the English Stage Company at the Royal Court Theatre. Both *Lear* and *Serjeant Musgrave's Dance* were premiered there, and *Roots* was taken up by the Court after its first production at the Belgrade Theatre in Coventry. All three writers, particularly at the beginning of their stage careers, have been associated with the Royal Court: Wesker's first six plays were produced there, almost all of Bond's until the mid-1970s, and three of Arden's in the late 1950s. The trilogy of which *Roots* is the second part – the others are *Chicken Soup with Barley* (1958) and *I'm Talking about Jerusalem* (1960) – was, like *Serjeant Musgrave's Dance*, subsequently revived by the theatre as part of a body of contemporary classics. In addition to our three authors, the Royal Court has been instrumental in the development of contemporary drama in Britain. Thus the nature of the Royal Court as an institution, its identity and its philosophy, provide an important context for our three plays.

Some historical background first. The English Stage Company was established in 1954, appointed George Devine as its first artistic director and occupied the Royal Court Theatre in 1955. The original impetus behind the foundation of the company was a reaction against the absence of intellectual substance and experiment in the mainstream British theatre, particularly that of the commercial West End. Apart from the Theatre Workshop at Stratford East, which under the direction of Joan Littlewood produced work by Brecht and Brendan Behan, there was, as Kenneth Tynan wrote in 1954, 'nothing in the London theatre that one dares discuss with an intelligent man [*sic*] for more than five minutes'.[2] Outside London, the Arts Theatre in Cambridge produced a repertoire which introduced the European avant-garde to the British stage. On the whole, however, the drama was overwhelmingly middle-class: lightweight, reassuring entertainment in the form of musicals, revues, boulevard comedies and thrillers. George Devine set out to change this state of affairs by attacking it on two fronts: by altering the role of the writer, and by targeting a different audience. Consider these remarks, the first from Tony Richardson, another Royal Court director; and the second by Devine himself:

> [the Royal Court] would show a repertoire of modern plays and the possibilities of modern theatre, and . . . would also present plays which hadn't been produced in England, with the belief – and it was absolutely only a belief at that time – that this would produce a kind of renaissance of writing inside England.[3]

> I was not strictly after a popular theatre à la Joan Littlewood–Roger Planchon, but a theatre that would be part of the intellectual life of the country . . . I was convinced the way to achieve my objective was to get writers, writers of serious pretensions, back into the theatre . . . For me it is a temple of ideas, and ideas so well expressed it may be called art. So always look for quality in the writing above what is being said.[4]

What do you notice about the emphasis here? What underlying notions of dramatic quality and value are assumed?

DISCUSSION

The emphasis is very much upon the *writing*; since its inception the Royal Court has identified itself as a 'writer's theatre'. Quality and seriousness are the key values. But what do these terms actually mean in this context, and what are their implications? Do they perhaps promote essentially *literary* criteria as the measure of theatrical worth? Such a mode of playwrighting would aim for certain types of subtlety and complexity, density of style and allusion, enduring qualities of permanence and universality. It also suggests a form of drama in which language, the spoken word, has a central, even authoritative significance. You might see the appeal of *Serjeant Musgrave's Dance* and *Lear* to the Royal Court in this light: perhaps the disruptive pantomime elements of the former play are compensated for by its 'poetic' qualities; while the Shakespearian dimensions of the latter locate it reassuringly within a respectable literary culture.

This emphasis, favouring 'quality' above 'what is being said', sets an aesthetic rather than a political agenda. At least at the beginning, the theatre was certainly associated with socialist politics: its identity was forged amid the Suez Crisis and the Soviet invasion of Hungary, events which resulted in a profound re-alignment of socialist politics in Britain; many Royal Court writers and directors in the 1950s and early 1960s were active in movements such as the Campaign for Nuclear Disarmament; it was at the centre of the struggle to abolish theatre censorship later in the decade. The original Royal Court writers and directors were also influenced by Brecht and the Berliner Ensemble. The Royal Court philosophy and identity was defined as radical in the sense that it rejected the cultural – and to a certain extent political – values of the traditional middle class. But the protest was funda-mentally aesthetic: the theatre never claimed to be socialist in philosophy or in practice. Its patronage of the uncommercial and the avant-garde meant that it was prepared to produce Beckett alongside Bond, and John Osborne alongside John Arden. But this ostensible neutrality, which reflects a liberal commitment to culture in general rather than to the competing ideological positions offered by the plays themselves, is in itself a significant political manoeuvre. It may be that the diversity and eclecticism of the resulting repertoire depoliticizes the political play. Writing in 1981, Edward Bond criticized this Royal Court policy:

It seems to me that you cannot any longer create art without socialism and that therefore it is not only nonsense to ask an actor to act in Beckett one night and in Brenton the next – it is also nonsense to expect the audience to enjoy one and then the other. If they did, we have to say that they don't understand either ... I am convinced that trying to do Beckett one week and Brenton the next would be absurd and culturally pernicious. It would encourage an Edwardian attitude to the playing-fields and battlefields of art, as if it were to be chosen as a new shirt is chosen, on grounds of taste, comfort and variety – and as if changing your life or creating justice were as easy.[5]

Do you agree with Bond's argument? What does it imply about the relationship between socialist drama and the existing theatrical apparatus, as exemplified by the Royal Court?

DISCUSSION

Bond is calling for the theatre to be organized on political rather than aesthetic lines, isn't he? From the liberal culturalist perspective, this may seem doctrinaire or authoritarian, but it seems to me to be entirely logical and honest: it is the liberal approach to theatre and culture that evades the issue of its own commitments. But, within the existing theatrical apparatus at least, such a theatre seems inconceivable, supposing as it does a commitment to socialism on all sides (including the controllers of funding and subsidy). And it seems fair to assume that in the current commercial theatre a large-cast, large-scale play like *Lear* seems destined either for the subsidized theatre or for amateur performance.

All three of our writers were confronted with this problem, and adopted varying tactics to cope with it. Bond has written a number of plays to be performed outside the dominant apparatus of the progressive subsidized theatre, which have included *The Tin Can People* (1984) – performed by Bread and Circuses, a small-scale socialist touring theatre company – and works written for amateur groups and university drama departments. Meanwhile, he has continued to have work produced by the major subsidized companies, the Royal Court, the National Theatre and the Royal Shakespeare Company. His strategy has been to increase the degree of personal artistic control over the production of his work: since the production of *The Woman* in the National's Olivier Theatre in 1978 he has almost invariably appointed himself as director of the first productions of his plays. Whether this is an adequate solution to the problems of cultural production that we have already identified I leave to you to judge.

Arnold Wesker's response to the contradictions generated by the attempt to produce socialist theatre within the bourgeois cultural establishment was to lead, in the early 1960s, to his involvement in the foundation of Centre 42, a broad-based arts organization that was, Wesker hoped, to be financed by the trade-union movement. Its name derived from Resolution 42 carried at the 1960 TUC Congress, which committed the labour movement in principle to funding and support for the arts. The aim was to increase popular involvement in the arts, and its philosophy was a mixture of the culturist ethos romantically articulated in *Roots*, where cultural enlightenment was something to be brought (or handed down) to the working class, and grassroots involvement. It combined art exhibitions, theatre and poetry, folk and jazz performances. The project started out by mounting regional arts festivals, then moved into the Roundhouse theatre, where it remained until its collapse in 1970. The promised support from the TUC had not materialized, and the centre had become increasingly dependent upon business and private sources for finance, which in effect completely undermined its entire purpose.

The careers of Bond and Wesker indicate how it is possible for socialist drama to be assimilated, albeit uneasily, into the theatrical mainstream. The course of John Arden's work tells a different story. As we have already seen, one of the most effective ways of depoliticizing radical drama is to reconstitute it as a modern classic. Thus, for example, the original political content of *Serjeant Musgrave's Dance*, which, as Arden pointed out, 'dealt with a massacre of civilians during a British Army colonial "peace-keeping" operation at the same time as a bitter colliery strike in England',[6] is diffused into unhistorical parable, into an idealistic pacificist gesture. Moreover, this play has been used not only by critics but also, according to Arden, by theatre producers, as a standard by which to repudiate the openly revolutionary content of his later work. In 1972, in the context of the shooting of thirteen civilians by British paratroopers in Northern Ireland, and of industrial struggle by mineworkers, he rewrote the play as *Serjeant Musgrave Dances On*, to be performed by the revolutionary socialist 7:84 Theatre Company. Arden was subsequently to identify the distinction between what the theatrical establishment in Britain regarded as 'a genuine Arden work' and his subsequent plays:

a 'genuine Arden work' in fact meant 'a play like *Serjeant*

Musgrave's Dance, which does not come to any very positive conclusion' – whereas *non-genuine Arden* would be 'Arden at last affirming from his own hard experience the need for revolution and a Socialistic society: and moreover convinced that his artistic independence and integrity will be strengthened rather than compromised by so *doctrinaire* a stance...'[7]

For Arden, the move from liberal concern to revolutionary action entailed a rejection of the political and aesthetic accommodations of his earlier work. But it also involved a decisive break with the dominant theatrical apparatus: in 1972, along with his collaborator, Margaretta D'Arcy, he abandoned the British theatre to devote his energies to community theatre projects in the Republic of Ireland.

This brings us, finally, to the question of the audience. The extract from the Edward Bond poem that heads this chapter conveys a sentiment that all three writers would endorse. Where they would differ is on how it is to be put into action. Let us return again to the Royal Court. In a trenchant analysis of that theatre as a cultural institution, the playwright and director, John McGrath, has argued that not only the majority of its audience but also its predominant ethos is overwhelmingly bourgeois, reflecting the tastes and values of the educated liberal middle class. The 'radical' potential of any drama performed within this dramatic and cultural milieu will, therefore, be severely constrained by the need to tailor it to the aesthetic and political requirements that this imposes. Arguing against the idea that 'in order to change the meaning or class-orientation of theatre, all you need to do is to change the content of *some* of what happens on the stage',[8] McGrath points out that the inescapable class nature of the dominant theatre institutions themselves means that socialist drama which operates within their auspices cannot actually directly address the *real* agent of revolution, the working class. Surely a genuinely socialist culture has to be directly and concretely engaged in the front line of political struggle? Otherwise, 'socialist drama' is inevitably compromised by the institutional framework:

> we can see clearly that when the 'post-Osborne' British dramatists set out to 'tell the story', to mediate contemporary reality, they were already inflecting towards an account that would be acceptable to the middle class. Much as they may have thought that they had introduced the authentic voice of the working class into the theatre, as I'm sure did Wesker, Alun Owen, Edward Bond, Arden and even Pinter, the message that voice was trying to carry was inevitably swamped by the many other tongues of the event.[9]

Do you think that this is true of the three plays that we have studied? What alternatives can you see to this situation? Do you agree that a genuinely radical socialist theatre must also be a popular, working-class theatre?

DISCUSSION

These are open questions: it is perhaps impossible, finally, to offer definitive conclusions about the probable or likely political impact of a theatre performance. While it is true that a first production of an Arden, Bond or Wesker play at the Royal Court, or a prestigious revival by the National Theatre or Royal Shakespeare Company, will be directed at a predominantly bourgeois audience, this does not necessarily mean that any revolutionary impetus will be entirely absorbed by the apparatus. Perhaps we should see the fashioning of a revolutionary cultural politics as a more diffuse and contradictory process than a one-to-one transaction between audience and stage. On the other hand, radical theatrical statements may remain abstract and gestural when they refer to a revolutionary class which is largely excluded from the cultural milieu which the plays inhabit.

A fuller account of the many and varied possibilities for socialist theatrical intervention, which range from the television play through Theatre in Education to agitprop, is beyond the scope and method of this study; it is sufficient here to note that the play itself is only one mode of socialist cultural intervention among many. But there is one aspect of McGrath's argument with which we might end: what is 'legitimate' theatre? Who defines it as such, and for whom? To an extent, the whole form and emphasis of this book mirrors dominant ideologies of theatre and drama. Predominantly text-based study reflects (but can also reflect upon) a powerful institutional bias, the emphases of literary culture and its academic and educational apparatus. Canonized as the set text or student edition, plays such as the three we have studied perhaps present an acceptable face of socialist theatre, a theatre that is safely contained within the parameters of dramatic literature. We began by moving into our three texts; we might end by moving outside and beyond them, into the arena of political struggle where they, and we, really belong: 'If we give them a key/They know if the key will open the door'. It is as simple as that. Isn't it?

Notes

Chapter 1 – Politics and Drama

1 Eric Keown, *Punch*, 28 October 1959.
2 *The Times*, 23 October 1959.
3 Harold Hobson, *Sunday Times*, 25 October 1959.
4 *Observer*, 25 October 1959.
5 David Roper, *Plays and Players*, July 1984.
6 A. Alvarez, *New Statesman*, 31 October 1959.
7 Hobson, *Sunday Times*, 25 October 1959.
8 John Arden, advertisement in the *New York Times*, 15 May 1966.
9 John Arden, 'Author's Preface' in *Two Autobiographical Plays* (Methuen, 1971), p. 17.
10 Ronald Hayman, *John Arden* (Heinemann, 1968), p. 29.
11 Hayman, p. 28.
12 John Russell Brown, 'John Arden: Artificial Theatre' in Brown, *Theatre Language* (Allen Lane, 1972).
13 Andrew Kennedy, *Six Dramatists in Search of a Language* (Cambridge University Press, 1975).
14 John Russell Taylor, *Anger and After: A Guide to the New British Drama* (Methuen, 1962), pp. 84–5.
15 Glenda Leeming, *John Arden* (Longman, 1974), p. 7.
16 Catherine Itzin, *Stages in the Revolution: Political Theatre in Britain since 1968* (Methuen, 1980), pp. 28–9.
17 Bertolt Brecht, 'Theatre for Pleasure or Theatre for Instruction' in John Willett (ed.), *Brecht on Theatre* (Methuen, 1964), p. 71.

Chapter 2 – Text and Performance

1 Gregory Dark, 'Production Casebook No. 5: Edward Bond's *Lear* at the Royal Court', *Theatre Quarterly*, 5 (1972), p. 23.
2 Herbert Zapf, 'Two Concepts of Society in Drama: Bertolt Brecht's *The Good Woman of Setzuan* and Edward Bond's *Lear*', *Modern Drama*, 31 (1988), p. 231.
3 David Hirst, *Edward Bond* (Macmillan, 1985), p. 132.
4 Keir Elam, *The Semiotics of Theatre and Drama* (Methuen, 1980), p. 139.
5 Raymond Williams, *Drama in Performance* (Penguin, 1972), p. 174.

Chapter 3 – Form and Meaning

1 It is worth noting that Beatie's gesture of independence at the end of the play is separation from the family meal table: her expression of victory has the poignant hint of an anorexic future. I am grateful to Nikki Goode for alerting me to these (probably unintentional) implications, as well as illuminating the structural and ideological significance of food throughout the play.
2 Irving Wardle, *The Times*, 9 May 1978.
3 Gareth Lloyd Evans, *The Guardian*, 26 May 1959.
4 Ronald Hayman, *Arnold Wesker* (Heinemann, 1970), pp. 31–41.
5 Charles Osborne, *Daily Telegraph*, 6 February 1959.
6 Émile Zola, 'Naturalism in the Theatre' in Eric Bentley (ed.), *The Theory of the Modern Stage* (Penguin, 1968), p. 367.
7 Raymond Williams, *Culture* (Fontana, 1981), p. 169.
8 J.L. Styan, *Modern Drama in Theory and Practice*, Vol. 1 (Cambridge University Press, 1981), pp. 149–50.
9 John Arden, 'Telling a True Tale', *Encore*, May 1960.
10 John Arden, interview in *Peace News*, 30 October 1963, reprinted in *Encore*, October 1965.
11 Albert Hunt, *Arden* (Methuen, 1974), p. 26.
12 Brecht, 'The Modern Theatre is the Epic Theatre' in John Willett (ed.), *Brecht on Theatre* (Methuen, 1964), p. 37.
13 Hunt, *Arden*, p. 24.
14 Arden, 'Telling a True Tale', p. 128.
15 Edward Bond, 'Author's Preface' in *Lear* (Methuen, 1972), p. lxvi.
16 Edward Bond, 'On Brecht: a letter to Peter Holland', *Theatre Quarterly*, 30 (1978), pp. 34–5.
17 Giles Gordon, *The Spectator*, 21 May 1983.
18 William Gaskill, *A Sense of Direction: Life at the Royal Court* (Faber, 1988), p. 121.
19 Gregory Dark, 'Production Casebook No. 5: Edward Bond's *Lear* at the Royal Court', *Theatre Quarterly*, 5 (1972), p. 22.

Chapter 4 – Language and Character

1 Arnold Wesker, interviewed by Simon Trussler in Charles Marowitz and Simon Trussler (eds), *Theatre at Work* (Methuen, 1967), p. 88.
2 Constantin Stanislavsky, *Building a Character*, trans. Elizabeth Hapgood Reynolds (Max Reinhardt, 1950), p. 113.
3 Catherine Belsey, *Critical Practice* (Methuen, 1980), p. 59.
4 William Gaskill, 'And the time of the great taking over', *Encore*, April 1962.
5 Edward Bond, *The Woman* (Methuen, 1979), pp. 127–9.
6 Ronald Hayman, *John Arden* (Heinemann, 1968), pp. 24–5.
7 Frances Gray, *John Arden* (Macmillan, 1982), p. 13.
8 Walter Benjamin, *Understanding Brecht* (New Left Books, 1977), p. 17.

Chapter 5 – Genre and Metadrama

1 Brecht frequently cited the Elizabethan drama and theatre as one of the models for his Epic Theatre. He saw the non-illusionist stagecraft as 'full of A-effects', and its drama as experimental and contradictory, embodying a materialist understanding of history. See the section on 'Shakespeare's Theatre' in Brecht, *The Messingkauf Dialogues*, trans. John Willett (Methuen, 1964), pp. 57–64.

2 Bond, interviewed by Simon Trussler, 'The long road to Lear', *Theatre Quarterly*, 5 (1972), p. 8.

3 Brecht, *The Messingkauf Dialogues*, p. 44.

4 John Arden, 'Telling a True Tale', *Encore*, May 1960, p. 128.

5 Katherine Worth, *Revolutions in Modern English Drama* (Bell, 1972), p. 127.

6 John Arden, 'Building the Play', *Encore*, July 1961.

7 T.C. Worsley, *Financial Times*, 31 July 1959.

8 Walter Allen, *New Statesman*, 11 July 1959.

9 Kenneth Tynan, *Observer*, 4 July 1959.

10 Raymond Williams, *The Country and the City* (Paladin, 1975), p. 9.

Chapter 6 – Theatres and Audiences

1 Edward Bond, 'The Art of the Audience' in *The Warehouse: A Writer's Theatre*, Dartington Theatre Papers, 3rd series, no. 8 (1979).

2 Kenneth Tynan, *Tynan on Theatre* (Penguin, 1964), p. 33.

3 Quoted in Terry Browne, *Playwright's Theatre* (Pitman, 1975), p. 33.

4 Quoted in Irving Wardle, *The Theatres of George Devine* (Jonathan Cape, 1978), p. 279.

5 Edward Bond, 'The Theatre I Want' in Richard Findlater (ed.), *At the Royal Court: 25 Years of the English Stage Company* (Amber Lane Press, 1981), pp. 122–3.

6 John Arden, *To Present the Pretence: Essays on the Theatre and its Public* (Methuen, 1977), p. 155.

7 Arden, *To Present the Pretence*, p. 158.

8 John McGrath, *A Good Night Out, Popular Theatre: Audience, Class and Form* (Methuen, 1981), p. 16.

9 McGrath, p. 16.

Suggestions for Further Reading

Chapter 1

Serjeant Musgrave's Dance is published in three editions: as a Methuen Modern Play (Methuen, 1960); as a Methuen Student Edition, which includes commentary, notes and production photographs, edited by Glenda Leeming (Methuen, 1982); and in Arden, *Plays: One* (Methuen, 1977). *Lear* is published as a Methuen Modern Play (Methuen, 1971) and Student Edition, edited by Patricia Hern (Methuen, 1983), and in Bond, *Plays: Two* (Methuen, 1978). The recommended editions of *King Lear* are the Arden Shakespeare, edited by Kenneth Muir (Methuen, 1972), or the New Cambridge Shakespeare, edited by Norman Holland (Cambridge University Press, 1990). *Roots* is published in *The Wesker Trilogy* (Penguin, 1964), reprinted with revisions as *Arnold Wesker: Volume One* (Penguin, 1981).

The original reviewers' responses to *Serjeant Musgrave's Dance* are sampled in *Arden on File*, compiled by Malcolm Page (Methuen, 1985). Selections from reviews of the first productions of *Lear* and *Roots* can be found in *Bond on File*, compiled by Philip Roberts (Methuen, 1985) and *Wesker on File*, compiled by Glenda Leeming (Methuen, 1985). The anthology *Postwar British Theatre Criticism*, edited by John Russell Taylor (Routledge & Kegan Paul, 1981) also reprints a number of reviews of the first production of *Roots*. Liberal and conservative critical responses to *Serjeant Musgrave's Dance* are exemplified by Ronald Hayman, *John Arden* (Heinemann, 1968), Michael Anderson, *Anger and Detachment* (Pitman, 1976) and by Glenda Leeming, *John Arden* (Longman, 1974); while socialist analyses are offered by Albert Hunt, *Arden: A Study of His Plays* (Methuen, 1974) and Frances Gray, *John Arden* (Macmillan, 1982). Selections of Arden's own theoretical writings on the relationship between theatre and politics are collected in *To Present the Pretence: Essays on the Theatre and its Public* (Methuen, 1977) and (with Margaretta D'Arcy) *Awkward Corners* (Methuen, 1988). The author's prefaces to *Two Autobiographical Plays* (Methuen, 1971) and to *Plays: One* are also illuminating. The theoretical writings of Bertolt Brecht are fundamental to any discussion of political theatre; a selection of these can be found in John Willett (ed.), *Brecht on Theatre* (Methuen, 1964). See in particular: 'The Modern Theatre is the Epic Theatre', 'Theatre for Pleasure or Theatre for Instruction', 'The Street Scene' and 'A Short Organum for the Theatre'. *The Messingkauf Dialogues*, edited by John Willett (Methuen, 1964), is also useful. For a discussion of the politics of critical common sense, see Terry Eagleton, *Literary Theory: An Introduction* (Basil Blackwell, 1983).

Chapter 2

The theories and methods of 'stage-centred', active reading of the dramatic text are dealt with in Marjorie Boulton, *The Anatomy of Drama* (Routledge & Kegan Paul, 1960); J.L. Styan, *The Elements of Drama* (Cambridge University Press, 1960); Raymond Williams, *Drama in Performance* (Penguin, 1972); and Peter Reynolds, *Drama: Text into Performance* (Penguin, 1986). Structuralist and semiotic approaches are accessibly introduced in Keir Elam, *The Semiotics of Theatre and Drama* (Methuen, 1980) and Martin Esslin, *The Field of Drama* (Methuen, 1987). For an illuminating account of the rehearsals for the Royal Court production of *Lear*, see Gregory Dark, 'Production Casebook No. 5: Edward Bond's *Lear* at the Royal Court', *Theatre Quarterly*, 5 (1972).

Chapter 3

For a guide to the general background to *Roots*, and the naturalistic tradition upon which it draws, see Raymond Williams, *Drama from Ibsen to Brecht* (1952; revised edition, Chatto and Windus, 1968); Williams, 'Social environment and theatrical environment: the case of English Naturalism' in Raymond Williams and Marie Axton (eds), *English Drama: Forms and Development* (Cambridge University Press, 1977). J.L. Styan's three-volume study, *Modern Drama in Theory and Practice* (Cambridge University Press, 1981), locates British drama of the 1950s and 1960s in its European context: Volume 1 deals with Realism and Naturalism, Volume 3 with Expressionism and Epic Theatre. Lilian Furst and Peter Skrine's *Naturalism* (Methuen, 1971) summarizes the philosophical and scientific background as well as the literary and dramatic tradition. Brecht is usually the starting point for most discussions of the Epic Theatre in Britain, and, apart from Brecht's own writings, a number of critical studies are of relevance to Arden and Bond. Walter Benjamin, *Understanding Brecht* (New Left Books, 1977) offers some basic definitions of Epic Theatre; John Willett, *The Theatre of Bertolt Brecht* (revised edition, Methuen, 1978), summarizes the key features of Brecht's theory and practice. Peter Thomson and Jan Needle's *Brecht* (Blackwell, 1981) concentrates mainly on Brecht's plays, but includes a discussion of his influence upon Bond. The British dimension of Brecht is also discussed by M. Germanou in 'Brecht and the English Theatre' in Graham Bartram and Anthony Waine (eds), *Brecht in Perspective* (Longman, 1982), by John Willett in 'Ups and downs of British Brecht' in Pia Kleber and Colin Visser (eds), *Re-interpreting Brecht: his influence on contemporary drama and film* (Cambridge

University Press, 1990), and by Christopher McCullough in 'From Brecht to Brechtian: estrangement and appropriation' in Graham Holderness (ed.), *The Politics of Theatre and Drama* (Macmillan, 1992). For a critical discussion of Brecht's theory and practice in the broader context of revolutionary theatre, see Augusto Boal, *Theatre of the Oppressed* (Pluto Press, 1979).

Formal developments in English drama of the 1950s and 1960s are surveyed in Katherine Worth, *Revolutions in Modern English Drama* (Bell, 1972), which has one chapter devoted to Bond; Ronald Hayman, *British Theatre Since 1955* (Oxford University Press, 1979); Laurence Kitchen, *Mid-Century Drama* (Faber, 1962); John Elsom, *Postwar British Theatre* (Routledge & Kegan Paul, 1977); John Russell Taylor, *Anger and After: A Guide to the New British Drama* (Methuen, 1962); Taylor, *The Second Wave* (Methuen, 1971); and Arnold Hinchliffe, *British Theatre 1950/70* (Blackwell, 1974). *The Encore Reader*, edited by Charles Marowitz, Tom Milne and Owen Hale (Methuen, 1965; reissued as *New Theatre Voices of the Fifties and Sixties*, Methuen, 1981) affords access to the contemporary debates about theatre and drama, reprinting articles from *Encore* magazine. *Roots*, and its relation to Naturalism, are discussed in Ronald Hayman, *Arnold Wesker* (Heinemann, 1970); Glenda Leeming and Simon Trussler, *The Plays of Arnold Wesker* (Gollancz, 1971); Glenda Leeming, *Arnold Wesker* (Longman, 1972) and *Wesker the Playwright* (Methuen, 1983). Michelene Wandor's *Look Back in Gender* (Methuen, 1987) has a chapter on Wesker's representation of gender roles and the family (it also has a chapter on *Serjeant Musgrave's Dance*); for a more general account of the representation of women in the theatre see Lesley Ferris, *Acting Women* (Macmillan, 1990). For an examination of Wesker's language, see John Russell Brown, 'Arnold Wesker: Theatrical Demonstration' in Brown, *Theatre Language* (Allen Lane, 1972); and Gareth Lloyd Evans, *The Language of Modern Drama* (Dent, 1977).

Stratford-upon-Avon Studies 4: Contemporary Theatre (Edward Arnold, 1961) contains essays on dramatic form in Wesker and Arden: Clifford Leech, 'Two Romantics: Arnold Wesker and Harold Pinter'; and G.W. Brandt, 'Realism and Parables (from Brecht to Arden)'. Brown, *Theatre Language*, and Worth, *Revolutions in Modern English Drama*, analyse Arden's formal innovations without bringing politics into the discussion; while Hunt, *Arden* and Gray, *John Arden* draw upon Brecht to relate form to revolutionary political content. The relationship between form, stage technique and political content in the plays of Bond is analysed in Tony Coult, *Edward Bond* (2nd edition, Methuen, 1979); Malcolm Hay and Philip Roberts, *Bond: A Study of his Plays* (Methuen, 1980); and Jenny S. Spencer, 'Edward Bond's Dramatic Strategies' in C.W.E. Bigsby (ed.), *Stratford-upon-Avon Studies 19: Contemporary English Drama* (Edward Arnold, 1981). David Hirst's *Edward Bond* (Macmillan, 1985) discusses *Lear* as the closest of Bond's early plays to Brecht's in scope and method; the link between Brecht and Bond is explored by Peter Holland in 'Brecht, Bond, Gaskill and the Practice of Political Theatre', *Theatre Quarterly*, 30 (1978). The same issue contains Bond's response to this article, 'On Brecht: a letter to Peter Holland'.

Bond's dramatic theory is also expounded in his preface to *The Bundle* (Methuen, 1978), and in the notes that accompany *The Woman* (Methuen, 1979), *The Worlds* (Methuen, 1980), and *Two Post-Modern Plays* (Methuen, 1990).

Chapter 4

For an exposition of Naturalistic techniques of character-building, see Constantin Stanislavsky, *An Actor Prepares* (1937; Methuen, 1980), *Creating a Role* (1961; Methuen, 1981), and *Building a Character* (Max Reinhardt, 1950), all translated by Elizabeth Hapgood Reynolds. The Naturalism of Wesker's dialogue is examined in Gareth Lloyd Evans, *The Language of Modern Drama* (Dent, 1977). The idea of individual self-fulfilment as a central dynamic in Wesker's plays is explored in Glenda Leeming, 'Articulacy and Awareness' in C.W.E. Bigsby (ed.), *Contemporary English Drama* (Edward Arnold, 1981). For Epic theories of acting see *Brecht on Theatre*: 'Criteria for Judging Acting', 'New Technique of Acting' and 'The Street Scene'. William Gaskill, the first director of many of Bond's plays, discusses from practical experience Bond's writing for actors in *A Sense of Direction: Life at the Royal Court* (Faber, 1988). Post-structuralist analysis of character and subjectivity can be found in Catherine Belsey, *Critical Practice* (Methuen, 1980).

Chapter 5

For the thinking behind Bond's appropriation of Shakespeare see the interview 'The long road to Lear', in *Theatre Quarterly*, 5 (1972), reprinted in Simon Trussler (ed.), *New Theatre Voices of the Seventies* (Methuen, 1980); and Malcolm Hay and Philip Roberts, *Bond: A Study of his Plays* (Methuen, 1980), where the evolution of the play, in particular its changing relationship to its sources, is traced through its early manuscript drafts. Bond reflects upon Shakespeare in the Introduction to *Plays: Two* (Methuen, 1978) and in his dramatization of Shakespeare's death, *Bingo* (Methuen, 1974). For critical discussions of the relationship between Bond and Shakespeare, see Ruby Cohn, *Modern Shakespeare Offshoots* (Princeton University Press, 1976); Michael Scott, *Shakespeare and the Modern Dramatist* (Macmillan, 1988); Alan Sinfield, '*King Lear* versus *Lear* at Stratford', *Critical Quarterly*, 24 (1982) and 'Making space: appropriation and confrontation in recent British plays', in Graham Holderness (ed.), *The Shakespeare Myth* (Manchester University Press, 1988). This critical anthology deals also with the more general questions of cultural and political authority that arise from Shakespeare's status within the literary and dramatic canon. A representative sample of conventional humanist readings of *King Lear* can be found in Frank Kermode (ed.), *King Lear: A Casebook* (Macmillan, 1969); an overview of the critical history of the play is provided by Anne Thompson in *The Critics Debate: King Lear* (Macmillan, 1988). The stage history of *King Lear* is documented in detail by J.S. Bratton in *Plays in Performance: King Lear* (Bristol Classical Press, 1987), which also discusses Bond's play.

Arden's use of popular dramatic forms is discussed by Albert Hunt in *Arden: A Study of His Plays* (Methuen, 1974) and by Frances Gray, *John Arden* (Macmillan, 1982), while Helena Forsas-Scott discusses the folk play and mummers' play elements in 'Life and Love and Serjeant Musgrave: An Approach to Arden's Play', *Modern Drama*, 26 (1983). Peter Davison, *Contemporary Drama and the Popular Dramatic Tradition in England* (Macmillan, 1982), documents the cultural resources from which Arden's dramaturgy draws. The contradictions within Wesker's Naturalism are discussed in Tom Costello, 'The Defeat of Naturalism in Arnold Wesker's *Roots*', *Modern Drama*, 21 (1978). For general theoretical accounts of self-reflexivity and metafiction, see Lionel Abel, *Metatheatre: A New View of Dramatic Form* (Hill and Wang, 1963); Patricia Waugh, *Metafiction* (Methuen, 1984); Linda Hutcheon, *Narcissistic Narrative* (Methuen, 1984) and Hutcheon, *A Theory of Parody* (Methuen, 1985). On the pastoral tradition, see William Empson, *Some Versions of Pastoral* (Penguin, 1966); Peter Mavinelli, *Pastoral* (Methuen, 1971); and Raymond Williams, *The Country and the City* (Chatto and Windus, 1964).

Chapter 6

General studies of the history of English theatre from the 1950s to the 1960s are found in Katherine Worth, *Revolutions in Modern English Drama* (Bell, 1972); John Elsom, *Postwar British Theatre* (Routledge & Kegan Paul, 1977); Ronald Hayman, *British Theatre Since 1955* (Oxford University Press, 1979); John Russell Taylor, *Anger and After: A Guide to the New British Drama* (Methuen, 1962), and Taylor, *The Second Wave* (Methuen, 1971), and Arnold Hinchliffe, *British Theatre 1950/70* (Blackwell, 1974). The class composition of the new audiences of the period, and the corresponding shifts of emphasis and approach in the drama itself, are analysed in Alan Sinfield, 'The Theatre and its Audiences' in Alan Sinfield (ed.), *Society and Literature 1945–1970* (Methuen, 1983). Arnold Wesker's involvement in Centre 42 is detailed in Frank Coppieters, 'Arnold Wesker's Centre Fortytwo: a Cultural Revolution Betrayed', *Theatre Quarterly*, 18 (1975). For the history of the Royal Court, see Terry Browne, *Playwright's Theatre* (Pitman, 1975); Richard Findlater (ed.), *At the Royal Court: 25 Years of the English Stage Company* (Amber Lane Press, 1981); Irving Wardle, *The Theatres of George Devine* (Jonathan Cape, 1978); Philip Roberts, *The Royal Court Theatre* (Routledge & Kegan Paul, 1986); Gresdna A. Doty and Billy T. Harbin (eds), *Inside the Royal Court Theatre, 1956–1981: Artists Talk* (Louisiana State University Press, 1990); Julian Hilton, 'The Court and its Favours' in C.W.E. Bigsby (ed.), *Contemporary English Drama* (Edward Arnold, 1981); and William Gaskill, *A Sense of Direction: Life at the Royal Court* (Faber, 1988). A trenchant critique of the cultural profile and politics of the Royal Court is offered by John McGrath in *A Good Night Out: Popular Theatre, Audience, Class and Form* (Methuen, 1981), which records the author's experience in working-class political theatre. Aspects of the fringe and alternative theatre movement are also documented in Albert Hunt, *Hopes for Great Happenings*

(Methuen, 1976); Catherine Itzin, *Stages in the Revolution: Political Theatre in Britain since 1968* (Methuen, 1980); Sandy Craig (ed.), *Dreams and Deconstructions: Alternative Theatre in Britain* (Amber Lane Press, 1980); David Edgar, *The Second Time as Farce: reflections on the drama of mean times* (Lawrence and Wishart, 1988); John McGrath, *The Bone Won't Break: On Theatre and Hope in Hard Times* (Methuen, 1990); John Arden, *To Present the Pretence* (Methuen, 1977); and John Arden and Margaretta D'Arcy, *Awkward Corners* (Methuen, 1988).

Index